YOU ARE STRONGER THAN YOU THINK

UNLEASH THE POWER TO GO BIGGER, GO BOLD,
AND GO BEYOND WHAT LIMITS YOU

JOEL OSTEEN

New York   Nashville

ALSO BY JOEL OSTEEN

A Fresh New Day Journal

All Things Are Working
for Your Good
*Daily Readings from All Things Are
Working for Your Good*

Blessed in the Darkness
Blessed in the Darkness Journal
Blessed in the Darkness Study Guide

Break Out!
Break Out! Journal
Daily Readings from Break Out!

Empty Out the Negative

Every Day a Friday
Every Day a Friday Journal
*Daily Readings from Every Day
a Friday*

Fresh Start
Fresh Start Study Guide

I Declare
*I Declare Personal Application
Guide*

Next Level Thinking
Next Level Thinking Journal
Next Level Thinking Study Guide
*Daily Readings from Next Level
Thinking*

Peaceful on Purpose
Peaceful on Purpose Study Guide
Peace for the Season

The Abundance Mind-set

The Power of Favor
The Power of Favor Study Guide

The Power of I Am
The Power of I Am Journal
The Power of I Am Study Guide
*Daily Readings from The Power
of I Am*

Think Better, Live Better
Think Better, Live Better Journal
*Think Better, Live Better Study
Guide*
*Daily Readings from Think Better,
Live Better*

Two Words That Will
Change Your Life Today

With Victoria Osteen
Our Best Life Together
Wake Up to Hope Devotional

You Are Stronger than
You Think
*You Are Stronger than You Think
Study Guide*

You Can, You Will
You Can, You Will Journal
*Daily Readings from You Can,
You Will*

Your Best Life Now
Your Best Life Begins Each Morning
Your Best Life Now for Moms
Your Best Life Now Journal
Your Best Life Now Study Guide
*Daily Readings from Your Best
Life Now*
*Scriptures and Meditations for
Your Best Life Now*
Starting Your Best Life Now

YOU ARE
STRONGER
THAN
YOU THINK

FaithWords
Hachette Book Group
1290 Avenue of the Americas, New York, NY 10104
faithwords.com
twitter.com/faithwords

First Edition: October 2021

FaithWords is a division of Hachette Book Group, Inc. The FaithWords name and logo are trademarks of Hachette Book Group, Inc.

The publisher is not responsible for websites (or their content) that are not owned by the publisher.

The Hachette Speakers Bureau provides a wide range of authors for speaking events. To find out more, go to www.hachettespeakersbureau.com or call (866) 376-6591.

Library of Congress Control Number: 2021939207

ISBN: 978-1-5460-4176-4 (hardcover); 978-1-5460-4178-8 (ebook); 978-1-5460-4177-1 (large print)

Printed in the United States of America

LSC-H

Printing 1, 2021

CONTENTS

YOU ARE
STRONGER
THAN
YOU THINK

CHAPTER ONE

You Are Stronger than You Think

We all face pressure in life and times when we could feel over-whelmed. The obstacle looks too big, we never dreamed we'd be dealing with a sickness, or we thought the trouble at work would be over by now. It's easy to feel as though it's too much, and we can't take it anymore. But the Scripture says, "God will not let you be tempted beyond what you can endure, but He will make a way of escape so that you will be able to bear it." When God designed you, He took into account everything you would face—every struggle, every unfair situation, every setback—and He put in you the strength, the courage, and the determination to withstand it. When you feel overwhelmed, as though the pressure is too much, it's because you're stronger than you think. You haven't discovered all that's in you. You'll never know how strong you really are until you face pressure that you've never faced. It may seem unbearable, but the fact that God allowed it means you can handle it.

God didn't say He would make a way of escape so you can run from it, or so you can avoid it. He said it was so you can bear it. You can look back at times when you didn't think you could go on, the pressure seemed unbearable, but somehow it didn't defeat you. You had the strength to get up another day, and you kept going when you didn't feel you had anything left. Why didn't it break you? Because you were stronger than you thought. God designed you to handle that pressure. He wouldn't have allowed you to get in that pressure if He hadn't already put in you what you needed to handle it. You will always be able to bear whatever comes your way.

I read about a little fish called the Mariana snailfish. It lives at the very bottom of the ocean, almost five miles underwater. No other fish can survive at that depth. The pressure at that depth is more than a thousand times the pressure at the surface. It would crush any other fish. But when God designed this snailfish, He made its bones flexible so they could withstand the pressure. These fish have special cells and a unique digestive system. Most fish have one gene to stabilize proteins, but this fish has five. Because they're designed to handle the pressure, they don't live burdened, struggling, or overwhelmed; they thrive there. In the same way, when God designed you, He knew what pressures you would face—financial pressure, relationship pressure, raising children pressure, dealing with an illness pressure. If that pressure was going to crush you, if it was going to be unbearable, God wouldn't have put you there. He doesn't make mistakes. Whatever you face, remind yourself that you can handle it. You've been designed for it. You wouldn't be at that depth if the pressure was going to defeat you.

Now you have to get in agreement with God. If you go around thinking, *This is too much. I can't raise these kids. This pressure at work is overwhelming,* that's going to defeat you. The Scripture says you are full of can-do power. You are well able to overcome opposition, to outlast adversity. But I've learned that can-do power doesn't do you any good if you have a can't-do mentality. Quit looking at all the things you can't do. Have a new perspective: *I can do all things through Christ who strengthens me. This obstacle may be big, but I can overcome it. This trouble is taking longer than I thought, but I can outlast it. This situation feels overwhelming, but I can handle it. I've been designed for it. I'm strong, I'm anointed, and I'm equipped.*

> I've learned that can-do power doesn't do you any good if you have a can't-do mentality.

Don't have a weak mentality. You weren't created to fall apart when pressure comes. You are stronger than you think. You are more favored than you think. You are more anointed than you think. Like God designed that small fish with special cells and special bones to withstand the pressure, how much more has God designed you with special strength, with courage, with fortitude, with stamina. When you start seeing yourself as strong, empowered, and well able, you won't live overwhelmed. You'll discover strength that you didn't know you had.

Mighty Hero, Stand Strong

This is what happened to Gideon in Judges 6. He was hiding in the winepress as he threshed wheat, afraid of the Midianites who had surrounded his city. You can imagine the pressure he was under, how he felt overwhelmed, worried, wondering what was going to happen. Just when it seemed like he couldn't bear it anymore, an angel

> Gideon didn't know what was in him.

showed up and said, "Mighty hero, the Lord is with you." Other translations say, "Valiant man of fearless courage." Gideon didn't feel like a mighty hero. He was hiding. He didn't feel courageous. He felt weak and intimidated. This angel was saying in effect, "Gideon, you are stronger than you think. You're letting this situation overwhelm you. You think it's unbearable, too much to handle, but I'm here to tell you that you have what it takes. You're courageous, you're talented, you're favored, and you're well able." Gideon didn't know what was in him. He saw what was around him—enemies that looked too big, opposition that seemed insurmountable. The angel showed up to remind him of what was in him.

The angel went on to say, "Gideon, you are to lead the people of Israel against the Midianites." Even though he saw an angel, Gideon wasn't convinced. He said, "Are you kidding? I come from the poorest family, and I am the least one in my father's house." He was saying, "You're calling me strong, you're calling me a hero, but do you know my background? Do you know where I come from? Do you see what I'm up against?" Gideon didn't understand that God won't let us get in a situation if He hasn't already equipped us for it. If it was going to be too much to bear, too big a challenge to defeat, God wouldn't have allowed it. The fact that you're in it means you can handle it. As with Gideon, you may not think so— the odds are against you, it feels overwhelming, you don't see a way out—but you are stronger than you think. You are more powerful than you think. The Most High God is breathing on your life. He's saying to you today, "Mighty hero, rise up. Mighty hero, stand strong. Mighty hero, you are well able."

You would think that after the angel called him a mighty hero, Gideon would be full of faith, ready to take new ground, but he still wasn't convinced. God could have thought, *Forget it, Gideon. If you don't know what you have, if you see yourself as weak, then I'll find somebody else.* But God never gives up on us. You may think of all the reasons why you can't overcome, why that problem is too big, and how it's unbearable, but God is going to keep calling you a mighty hero. He's going to keep telling you that you're stronger than you think. He's going to keep pushing you forward, showing you signs of His favor.

Gideon and one of his men snuck down into the enemy's camp to see what was going on. Several armies had united with the Midianites to fight the Israelites. Gideon only had three hundred men. It seemed impossible. But just as they crept up to the camp, they overheard one of the Midianites telling about a dream that he had. The other Midianite said, "I know exactly what that dream means. God has given Gideon and the Israelites victory over us." When Gideon heard that, something came alive inside. He returned to camp, and he shouted to his men, "Get up! The Lord has given us the victory." He no longer felt weak, overwhelmed, and intimidated. He knew he was well able. At midnight, they attacked the enemy armies, and even though they were greatly outnumbered, Gideon and the Israelites won the victory.

Discover What's in You

I don't think we'd be talking about Gideon if the angel had not told him that he was stronger than he thought. If the angel had not called him a mighty hero, if he had not challenged him to see himself differently, Gideon would have missed his destiny. You're not reading this by accident. God is saying to you that you're stronger than you think. You're bigger than what you're up against. You were created to overcome, born with what you need to defeat what's

> *You have to go by what you know, not by what you feel.*

trying to stop you. You may feel weak, intimidated, and overwhelmed. That's okay. God made us with feelings. I'm not saying to not feel things. I'm saying to not let your feelings have the final say. Don't let your feelings run your life. You have to go by what you know, not by what you feel. When you feel weak, you need to say, "I am strong." When you feel overwhelmed, you need to say, "I can do all things through Christ." When you feel intimidated, you need to say, "I am a mighty hero." When the pressure feels too much, you need to say, "I can handle it. I'm well able to bear it."

It's significant that Gideon heard what the enemy in the Midianite camp was saying about him. That's what convinced him to see himself the right way. If you could hear the enemy talking about you, he'd be saying, "That's William. Don't mess with him. He serves the Most High God. That's Maria, and that's Susie. You better be careful, because they're powerful, they're favored, and they're strong." Sometimes the enemy knows who we are more than we know who we are. God is not only saying that you are stronger than you think, but even the enemy is saying, "If they find out who they are, surely they will defeat us. If they realize they are a mighty hero, we are no match for them." Are you seeing yourself the right way? Have you discovered what's in you? That situation that seems overwhelming, that pressure that feels unbearable, it's not there to defeat you but to help you discover strength that you didn't know you had. You're not weak or at a disadvantage; you are a mighty hero. You are a man or a woman of fearless courage.

The pressure on you from the outside may be great. Other people may not be able to take it, but God knew you would face it. That's why, as with that little snailfish, He's already giving you even more than what you need to just survive. To survive is one thing, when we just make it through life, burdened down, and feeling it's unbearable. You weren't created to survive but to thrive. When things come that should be unbearable, you've tapped into strength that you didn't know you had. You still give God praise, you still shine at work, and you still accomplish big dreams. Don't go your whole life and never discover what's in you. You are stronger than you think.

You Have Can-Do Power

Think about a little seed. It's just a quarter of an inch long, doesn't look like much. When you bury that seed in the ground, the dirt that's on top of it is thousands of times heavier, far more powerful. The little seed could think, *Just my luck. I was doing fine, then someone put me in this dirt. Someone buried me.* But what that seed knows is that God already took into account that one day it would be buried, that one day it would feel overwhelmed and be surrounded by pressure and forces that were much greater. So God put in that seed supernatural life, supernatural strength, supernatural ability. After it's

> *It's not the size of what you're up against. What matters is what the Creator put in you.*

buried, been trapped in the dark, and it looks as though it's over, that seed will germinate. It will open up and somehow begin to push the dirt out of the way. It was designed to be buried; it was designed to have dirt put on it. God knew the seed would face opposition that looked much bigger, which is why He put in it the strength to push up dirt, strength to move something many times stronger out of its way. God was showing us that it's not the size of what you're up against. What matters is what the Creator put in you. Don't be intimidated by how big the opposition is, by how bad the medical report looks, or by how powerful the people are who are against you. Like that seed, you have the life of Almighty God. You have the favor of God. You have can-do power. You are stronger than you think.

When that seed is buried, I can hear the dirt laughing and saying, "You're done now. You don't have a chance. I'm so much more powerful than you." The seed could panic, live overwhelmed, and say, "What am I going to do?" But this seed knows a secret. It says, "Hey, Mr. Dirt, I may look small, and I know I'm at a disadvantage right now. I know you're much bigger, but I'm not worried. I'm stronger than I look. I'm more powerful than I appear. I have something in me that's not ordinary, that's not common. I have the life of Almighty God." The dirt says, "Big deal. I'm still hundreds of times more powerful than you." But in a few weeks, the little seed opens, and the first shoot from the seed begins to push the dirt back, and push it back, and push it back. Before long, the shoot from the seed has come up out of the ground, and now it's a beautiful bush with blooming flowers.

In the same way, when things look as though they're going to overwhelm you, as though they're too much to bear, remember this phrase: You are stronger than you think. God knew it was coming. He's already put things inside that you can't see right now, but at the appointed time you're going to push back the dirt. You're going to come out of what's holding you back, but not like you were. You're going to bloom. You're going to blossom, go to new levels, and accomplish greater goals. Don't be fooled by the dirt. The dirt is getting you ready to flourish. There are things in your destiny that can only happen with the dirt. If you weren't buried, so to speak, you would never see what's in your seed. You wouldn't reach your potential.

You can keep an apple seed on a shelf for years. It looks nice. It doesn't have to get dirty, doesn't have to be uncomfortable, but that seed would never become what it was created to be. There are apple orchards in that one seed, but it will never produce a single apple without the dirt. The challenge is that when we get dirt on us, when we face things we don't understand and it feels overwhelming, it's easy to get discouraged, give up on our dreams, and live sour. "God, why is this happening?" That's going to keep our

> *There are apple orchards in that one seed, but it will never produce a single apple without the dirt.*

seed from germinating. The right attitude is: *This dirt is not stopping my destiny; it's taking me into my destiny.* God wouldn't have allowed the dirt if it was going to keep you from your purpose. The problem may look too big, the sickness looks too great, the trouble is not turning around. Can I tell you that you are stronger than you think? You can endure more than you think. That dirt is not going to defeat you; it's going to promote you.

Tap into Your Full Potential

In Numbers 11, Moses felt overwhelmed. He was leading the Israelites through the desert, some two million people, toward the Promised Land. They were complaining, "We're tired of eating the same food. We liked it better in Egypt. Why did you bring us out here in the desert?" Moses said, "God, why did You lay the burdens of all these people on me? They're not my children. I'm not able to bear this on my own. It's too heavy for me." He felt so pressured and so stressed that he added, "God, I would rather that You kill me than have me carry this heavy load." It felt unbearable. He couldn't take it anymore. God told him to call seventy men, seventy elders of the people, who could help him. God said to Moses, "I will take some of the spirit that's on you and put it on these men. They will help you carry the burden." One principle is to delegate, because you can't do everything by yourself. But it's interesting that God said He was going to take "some of the spirit" that was on Moses and put it on these men. Do you see how strong Moses was? Even though he couldn't do the work of all seventy, God said, "You have so much potential, you have so much you haven't tapped into, that I'm going to take from you and give it to them."

Imagine God taking from what's in you and giving it to seventy people, and you are still able to do great things. That's how strong you are. That's how powerful you are. That's how anointed you are. I want you to see yourself as a mighty hero, as someone who's well able. The reason you face big challenges is because

> *The reason you face big challenges is because you have a big destiny.*

you have a big destiny. The reason you have great obstacles is because you have greatness in you. The reason the pressure feels overwhelming is because you are stronger than you think. That difficulty is an opportunity for you to discover what's in you. This won't happen if you're weak, defeated, and saying, "I can't take it anymore. It's too much for me." If that was true, then God made a mistake when He designed you, or He accidentally put you in an environment that you couldn't handle. No, God doesn't make mistakes. The pressure is showing you how strong you are, how much you can handle. That's getting you ready for how high God is going to take you. He's preparing you for new levels, for greater influence, for unprecedented favor.

When I was growing up, we had a dog by the name of Scooter. My father used to ride his bike through the neighborhood, and Scooter would run alongside him. He was so proud of Scooter, who was a big German shepherd, strong and powerful. Scooter would take off ahead of my father and run through the neighbors' yards, check everything out, as though he were the king of the road. One day as they were riding, a little bitty Chihuahua saw Scooter coming down the street and started barking and barking. Scooter didn't think twice, but he took off toward that dog full speed, as though he was saying, "How dare you bark at me!" My father thought, *Oh no! Scooter is going to tear into that dog. One paw on him and that little dog will be done.* He sped up to try to calm Scooter down. The closer that Scooter got, the louder that dog barked. Finally Scooter got right up to him, the big showdown. My father was waiting for Scooter to show the Chihuahua who was boss, but Scooter rolled over on his back, put up all four legs in the air, as though he was saying, "I give up. Please don't hurt me." My father said, "I was so embarrassed by Scooter that I turned around and went home." Scooter was a lot bigger on the outside than he was inside. That little Chihuahua may have been small in size, but he was stronger than he looked, more powerful than he looked. I've learned that it's not the size of the problem, it's the size of the person.

My father was ashamed of Scooter, but I wonder how many times our heavenly Father looks down at us and says, "Why are you rolling over and putting up all fours? Why are you giving up, being overwhelmed, thinking you can't handle it, when I've called you a mighty hero,

> *Why are you rolling over and putting up all fours?*

when I've given you can-do power, when I've surrounded you with favor, when I've armed you with strength for every battle, when I'm going before you and making crooked places straight, when I've designed you to withstand any pressures that come against you." If you want to make God proud, stand strong, be courageous, think like a champion, talk like an overcomer, praise when you could be complaining, declare victory when all you see is defeat, and expect favor when it seems impossible. God has awesome things in your future, but there will be awesome challenges in your future. To reach your destiny, you have to discover what's in you. Every time you realize that you're stronger than you think, and you overcome, you outlast, and you endure, that strength is going to be instrumental for the next challenge, for the next dream. That's preparing you for the amazing things God has in store.

You Have the Life of Almighty God

David was a teenager, taking care of his father's sheep in the shepherds' fields. One day he took a supply of food to his three brothers who were in the army. When he arrived at the camp, he heard Goliath taunting the Israelite soldiers. Something rose up in him. He told King Saul that he wanted to fight Goliath. They all tried to talk him out of it, telling him that he was too small, not qualified, that he had no experience, but David was determined. When Goliath saw how small David was, he began to laugh and said, "Am I a dog that you come at me with a stick?" He was saying, "Is this the best you've got?" David looked at Goliath and said in effect, "I may be small, but I'm stronger than I look. I'm more powerful than I look. I'm more experienced than I look." David took his slingshot and with one stone brought down Goliath.

You may have some Goliaths telling you what you can't do. "You're not strong enough to break that addiction. You can't beat that sickness. You'll never accomplish that dream. You're not big enough." You have to do as David did and tell Goliath, "I may look small, but I'm stronger than you think. You haven't seen the best of me. You haven't seen the courage, the fortitude, or the greatness. You just see a Gideon. What you don't realize is that you're looking at a mighty hero." That problem is not going to defeat you, that trouble is not how your story ends, and that loss is not going to define you. You're going to discover things in you that you didn't know you had. I believe even now strength is rising up,

> *You're going to discover things in you that you didn't know you had.*

courage is rising up, dreams are coming back to life. You're about to see God do things that you couldn't do, turn situations around that look permanent, and open doors that no person can shut.

When I was ten years old, I played Little League Baseball. I was very small when I was growing up, always the shortest one on the team. One day when I got up to bat, the coach on the other team came out of the dugout and started waving his arms and shouting to the outfielders, "Come in closer! Come in closer!" It was as though he was saying, "This guy up to bat is a loser. Look how small he is. He can't hit." He made such a big scene that everyone in the stands was watching him. Something rose up in me. I thought, *You don't know who you're talking about. You don't know what I'm capable of.* The pitcher threw the first pitch, and I swung with all my might. That ball went over everyone's head and with one bounce it hit the fence. I felt like José Altuve. I was so fast that I rounded the bases for an inside-the-park home run. The next time I came up to bat, the same coach came out of the dugout, but this time he was waving his arms the other way and shouting, "Back up! Back up! Back up!" What happened? I was stronger than he thought.

I believe the enemy has misjudged you. He thinks you're a lightweight—you're too small, at a disadvantage, overwhelmed; life's been tough. Why don't you step up and show what's in you? Why don't you shake off the negative voices, quit listening to the Goliaths that are taunting you, quit believing the obstacle is too big, and show this world who you really are? There's a mighty hero waiting to come out. There's a giant killer. There's a history maker. There's an overcomer. You may have some dirt on you, you're going through challenges, but that dirt can't hold you down. You have the life of Almighty God. You've been designed for this time, equipped for what you're facing, empowered to fulfill your destiny. Now don't live with a can't-do mentality when you have can-do power. Get in agreement with God. If you do this, I believe and declare that you're about to discover strength, courage, ability, and favor like you've never seen. You're not just going to survive, you're going to thrive. You're going to overcome every obstacle, defeat every enemy, and accomplish every dream.

CHAPTER TWO

Invite God into Your Difficulties

Most of the time when we're facing a difficulty, we're praying, "God, get me out of this challenge. Get me out of this trouble at work, get me out of this financial setback, get me out of this sickness." There's nothing wrong with that, but before you get out, you have to invite God in. Sometimes the miracle is not in getting out, it's in what God is going to do in the situation. Instead of just praying, "God, get me out," why don't you start praying, "God, come into this hospital room while I take the treatment, come into this trouble at work where the people are unfair, come into this anxiety that I'm dealing with"? What's more powerful than God bringing you out is when God comes in and begins to change things. He comes in and gives you favor despite who's trying to push you down. He comes in and gives you strength that you can't explain. He comes in and gives you the grace to outlast what should stop you.

If you're only focused on God bringing you out, you're going to be frustrated, because God doesn't do things on our timetable. Sometimes it takes longer than we think. When you ask God to come in, you can be at rest. "God, I know You're right here with me. You're ordering my steps, and nothing can snatch me out of Your hands. At the right time, You'll get me to where I'm supposed to be." You don't have to fight everything or live frustrated and not be able to sleep at night. That happens when you're only focused on getting out, because God is waiting to come in. When you ask Him to come in, you're saying, "God, don't just change the situation, change me. Help me to not just go through this but to grow through it. Help me to learn, help me to develop greater confidence, increase my faith, and let my character come up higher." If God delivered you out of everything instantly, you would never reach your potential. God is working in the trouble. He's working in that situation that's uncomfortable.

Sometimes God is not bringing you out yet because He wants the odds to be against you in a bigger way, so when He brings you out, it's a greater miracle. The enemy whispers, "God doesn't even hear your prayers. Nothing is ever going to change." The truth is that God is setting you up to show Himself strong in your life. When He brings you out, people won't be able to deny the favor that's on your life.

With You Through the Floods

God says through the prophet Isaiah, "When you go through the waters, I will be with you. When you go through the rivers, they will not overwhelm you. When you walk through the fire, you will not be burned." It's interesting that He didn't say, "I'll keep you out of every fire. You won't have to face any famines." He says these challenges are going to come, that there will be adversities and things we don't understand. But the whole key to this verse is when He says, "I will be with you *in* the flood, *in* the fire, and *in* the famine." Are you trying to get out of something that God is going to take you through? Are you fighting the process, wondering why it happened? "God, I can't take this anymore." Everything will change if you start inviting God into the fire. He promised He'll be with you. Maybe He's just waiting for your invitation.

The right attitude is: *God, I believe You're going to bring me out, but in the meantime, I'm asking You to come into this struggle in my health, come into this loss that I'm going through, come into this depression that's trying to stop me.* When you invite Him into the difficulty, you'll feel Him breathing in your direction, enabling you, empowering you, favoring you. Is it a greater testimony that God kept you out of the fire or that God came with you into the fire and brought you through it? And which of these two paths allows you to emerge stronger, more confident, more capable? We all want to get out of trouble, out of adversities, but don't get so caught up in getting out that you forget to ask God to come in.

> *Are you trying to get out of something that God is going to take you through?*

David says in Psalm 23, "Though I walk through the valley of the shadow of death, I will fear no evil because You are with me." When you know God is with you, when you've invited Him into your situation, you'll have a smile in the middle of the difficulty, you'll have a song of praise in the prison like Paul and Silas did. You won't be complaining about the trouble or worried about how it's going to work out. You'll have peace in the midst of the storm. David didn't live afraid even though he went through valleys and all kinds of adversities because he understood this principle: to invite God into the trouble. He wasn't waiting to get out, because He knew God was right there with him.

If you're only praying "God, get me out," you'll be frustrated until it changes. "I can't enjoy my life because I have a child who's off course. I'm dealing with this sickness, and my finances are down. When it all turns around, I'll have a good attitude." You're waiting for God to get you out, while God is waiting for you to invite Him in. You

> *You're waiting for God to get you out, while God is waiting for you to invite Him in.*

have to do as David did and say, "Lord, thank You that You're with me in this valley. I'm not going to live afraid or worried. I know You're in control. I may not see a way, but I know You have a way." Instead of just trying to get out of the valley, out of the fire, out of the trouble, start praying, "God, come in. Let me feel Your presence in the fire. Show me Your greatness in this trouble." Then you'll have a peace that passes understanding, a hope when you should be distraught, and a joy when you could be discouraged.

With You in the Fire

In Daniel 3, three Hebrew teenagers wouldn't bow down in worship to King Nebuchadnezzar's golden idol. The king was so furious that he threatened to throw them into a fiery furnace. The teenagers said, "King, we're not worried because we know our God will deliver us." This made the king even angrier. He had the guards heat the fire seven times hotter than normal. The fire would have killed anyone at the regular temperature. Why did God have the king heat it seven times hotter? So it would be a bigger miracle. God wanted the odds to be even greater against them.

The fact is, God could have kept them out of the fire. He's God. He parted the Red Sea, and He opened blind eyes. It wouldn't have been any problem for Him to change the king's mind, or to have the teenagers escape, or to send a big earthquake as He did to open the prison doors for Paul and Silas. But God doesn't deliver us from every fire. Sometimes He'll take you through the fire. The good news is that He knows how to make you fireproof. People don't determine your destiny. Bad breaks can't stop God's plan for your life. Sickness, addictions, and unfair situations don't have the final say. Don't get discouraged because God didn't keep you out of the fire. God doesn't stop every negative situation. He uses these adversities to move us into our destiny.

The good news is that He knows how to make you fireproof.

We won't know His power if we're never thrown into a fire. You won't know He is a healer if you never face an illness. You won't know He can move mountains if you never face a big obstacle. Quit complaining about what you're up against; it's not a surprise to God. The opposition may have turned up the heat seven times hotter than normal, but they didn't do that without God's permission. He's not just in control of your life, He's in control of your enemies. Instead

When He's with you, you can't be defeated. You and God are a majority.

of complaining about the fire, invite Him into the fire. When He's with you, you can't be defeated. You and God are a majority. He's a supernatural God. He's not limited by fires, by floods, by famines. What should take you out can't defeat you. What should overwhelm you can't stop your destiny.

Instead of fighting these things that aren't fair, things that you don't understand, you have to realize that God has a purpose for it. The purpose is not so you will be miserable and live frustrated and worried. The purpose is so He can show His glory through you, so other people can see His power and favor on your life. Without great tests, you won't have a great testimony. Without big battles, you won't have big victories.

With You in Times of Trouble

The three Hebrew teenagers said to Nebuchadnezzar, "We know our God will deliver us." They made that statement of faith. Then they said something even more powerful: "But even if He doesn't, we're still not going to bow down." That's the kind of people that gives the enemy a nervous breakdown. It's when you can say, "God, this is what I'm believing for. This is what I'm hoping will happen. But even if it doesn't work out my way, I'm still going to give You praise. I'm still going to be good to others. I'm still going to pursue my dreams." That kind of attitude gets God's attention. You're saying, "God, not my will but let Your will be done."

Too often we put conditions on God and conditions on our prayers. "God, I'll be happy if my boss moves to the backside of Mars. When you get him out of my life, I'll have a good attitude."

Have you ever thought that God is using that person to do a work in you, to grow you up, to develop your character, to teach you to love those who are not very lovable? Instead of saying, "God, get me out of this situation," I'm asking you to pray, "God, come into this situation. Help me to have a good attitude and help me to do the right thing when the wrong thing is happening." It's very powerful when you can say, "God, if my boss never moves, if he's

> *Have you ever thought that God is using that person to do a work in you, to grow you up, to develop your character, to teach you to love those who are not very lovable?*

here until I go to Heaven, I thank You that You've given me the strength to overcome, the power to be happy in the midst of difficulties. I'm not going to let a person, a sickness, or an injustice to take my joy." Now you're growing and coming up higher. Sometimes God is waiting for you to pass the test and then He's going to bring you out.

King Nebuchadnezzar had the guards tie the teenagers' hands and feet with cords. When they threw them into the furnace, it was so hot that the guards were instantly killed. It looked as though it was the end for these teenagers, but people don't have the final say. Nothing can snatch you out of God's hands. If it's not your time to go, you're not going to go. In a little while, the king came to check on them. He looked into the mouth of the furnace and said, "Didn't we throw three men bound into the fire? I see four men loosed, and one looks like the Son of God."

God may not deliver you from the fire, but don't worry, He'll come in the fire with you. He'll help you overcome what looks impossible. What would have taken other people out won't have any effect on you. The illness should have been the end, the medical report said you were done, but like with my mother's battle with cancer, God got in the fire with you, and here you are still going strong. When you lost that loved one, or when that person walked away, the heartbreak should have soured your life, but look at you, still moving forward, doing great things, fulfilling your purpose. How can that be? God walked in the fire with you.

> *God may not deliver you from the fire, but don't worry, He'll come in the fire with you. He'll help you overcome what looks impossible.*

The Scripture says, "God is a very present help in times of trouble." We know that God is always with us, but when you're in difficulties, if you invite Him in, you'll feel His presence in a greater way. You'll be aware that you are not alone. You won't live frustrated because you were thrown into a fire. You'll stay at peace, knowing that the fourth man is right there with you. The God who controls the fire, the God who speaks to storms, the God who restores, who heals, and who pays you back for the injustice is watching over you, protecting you, and ordering your steps.

With You in the Difficulty

In Exodus 33, Moses was in a difficult situation. The people of Israel had just been judged for worshipping a golden calf in the wilderness, and he didn't know how things were going to work out. I'm sure he was tempted to be discouraged by their disobedience, by how big their enemies were as they moved ahead, and how impossible his dream looked. But God said to him, "Moses, My Presence will go with you. I will give you rest, and everything will be fine for you."

Maybe you're up against some challenges; some things haven't turned out the way you thought. You prayed for God to keep you out of the fire, but it didn't happen your way. You're wondering how you're going to beat that sickness, or how your family is ever going to be restored. God is saying to you what He said to Moses: "I'm going with you. You're not in the fire by yourself. I have you in the palms of My hands. I'm fighting your battles." That obstacle may be too big for you, but it's not too big for our God. Right now He's pushing back forces of darkness. He's keeping the fire from burning you. He's not letting you drown in those waters. He's your protector, your deliverer, your way maker, your provider, and your healer. You don't have to do this in your own strength, and you don't have to figure it all out. You're not going to know all the details. You have to walk by faith and not by sight.

> *That obstacle may be too big for you, but it's not too big for our God. Right now He's pushing back forces of darkness.*

> *How we approach our difficulties makes all the difference whether we come through them unharmed, not burned, and without even the smell of smoke, or we get stuck in them.*

When King Nebuchadnezzar had the teenagers tied up, they could have been panicked, stressed out, and said, "God, this isn't fair." Instead, they understood this principle: "God may not keep us out of the fire, but if we go into the fire, He'll go with us. We're not going alone." They didn't fall apart; they stayed in peace. They knew what God had told Moses centuries before: "Everything will be fine for you." I can imagine how different this story could have been if they had been bitter and frustrated and said, "We're doing the right things, and look what good it does. We get thrown into a furnace." Maybe we wouldn't be reading about them, because maybe the fourth man wouldn't have shown up. How we approach our difficulties makes all the difference whether we come through them unharmed, not burned, and without even the smell of smoke, or we get stuck in them.

If you are in a fire now, this is not the time to complain or the time to just pray that God will get you out. More than ever you need to say, "Father, thank You that You're in this fire with me. Thank You that no weapon formed against me will prosper. Thank You that what was meant for my harm You are turning to my advantage. I'm not going to worry. I'm going to trust. I believe that everything is going to be fine for me just as You said."

Here's how good God is. The king said, "Didn't we throw three men bound in the fire? I see four men loosed." When the teenagers came out, the only thing the fire had burned was the cords that had been holding them back. Their clothes were fine, their hair was fine, their skin was fine. Only the cords were burned. When you come out of that difficulty, the only things that are going to be gone are the limitations that were holding you back. The fire is going to burn off the fear, burn off the intimidation, burn off relationships that were pulling you down, burn off negative mind-sets. You're going to come out free, bold, confident, healthy, promoted, victorious, and ready to fulfill your destiny.

With You in the Mistreatment

I know an executive at a large company who was disliked by the people in management above him. He's very talented, which intimidated them, so they did their best to keep him down. He was upset about what was going on, trying to figure out what he could do to overcome them. For several months he came for prayer during our services, telling me how it was getting worse and wondering when God was going to turn it around. The stress was causing a strain on his marriage, and he was starting to get run-down physically. I told him what I'm telling you: "You're just praying, 'God, get me out.' You need to start praying, 'God, come into this situation and help me to shine where I am, give me the grace to bloom where I'm planted, to have a good attitude even though it's not changing.'" He changed his approach and quit worrying about when it was going to change, knowing that God was with him in the fire, fighting his battles.

When I saw him about two years later, he was as peaceful as can be, had a smile on his face, and a great attitude. I thought everything must have turned around. But he said, "Joel, the same people are still there, doing the same things. They haven't changed, but I've changed. I don't let them steal my joy, and I don't live stressed out. I'm at peace in the midst of the storm. I'm enjoying my life despite how they treat me. I do the right thing even though they don't give me the credit." That's passing the test. That's showing God that you're not going to just be happy if He brings you out, but you're going to shine even if it doesn't happen your way.

You're going to be your best even though it's not changing on your timetable. That's inviting God into the fire. It's not just "God, get me out," but "God, give me the strength to be here with a good attitude."

I saw him again in the church lobby about three months after that. This was about three years after he had first come for prayer. His company had recently been sold, and the new owners let go of all the management team except for him. He was the only executive they kept. He said, "Joel, now I'm running the whole company. I'm the one in charge." God knows how to vindicate you. God knows how to bring you out of the difficulty. The question is, are you inviting Him into the difficulty? When you're in the fire, you can't complain or be discouraged and say, "This isn't right. God, get me out." Try a different approach. "God, come into this fire with me. Help me to do the right thing, change me where I need to change, and burn off the things that are holding me back."

You have to shine where you are, have a song of praise when you could be complaining, and keep a smile when you feel like being sour. It's not easy but keep reminding yourself that the Creator of the universe, the Most High God, is right in that fire with you. He sees what you're up against. He knows what's not fair, the hurts, the disappointments, the lonely nights. When you dig down deep and do the right thing, you're going to feel a supernatural strength, a power that helps you do what you can't do on your own.

> *When you dig down deep and do the right thing, you're going to feel a supernatural strength, a power that helps you do what you can't do on your own.*

With You in the Injustice

This is what Joseph did. When he was a young man, he was betrayed by his brothers and sold into slavery. He worked for a high-ranking military official in Egypt named Potiphar. Joseph had every right to be bitter and upset. His dreams were shattered. He was away from his family, living in a foreign country, and didn't know anyone. But you never read that Joseph complained. He just kept being his best where he was. He was so exceptional at all he did that Potiphar put him in charge of his whole house. The Scripture says, "The Lord was with Joseph, and he was successful in everything he did." Joseph did what I'm asking us to do. He didn't pray, "God, get me out of this trouble, and then I'll have a good attitude." He prayed, "God, come into this trouble with me, help me to shine, help me to stand out." One verse later, it says, "Potiphar saw that the Lord was with Joseph." My question is, can people see that the Lord is with you in the fire? Are you being your best when circumstances aren't fair? Are you shining when you could be complaining?

Later, Joseph was put in prison for something that he didn't do. The Scripture says, "The Lord was with Joseph there too." In the prison, in the betrayal, in the injustice, God was still right there. It's significant that the Scripture tells us three times within a few verses from each other that the Lord was with Joseph. We got it the first time, but God wanted us to see this principle: When you invite God into the fire with you, you're going to have a favor that pushes you up when life is trying to push you down. You're going to have a strength to excel when you should be slacking off, a power to overcome what should defeat you. Finally, after thirteen years of being in the fire, God brought Joseph out and made him second-in-command in Egypt.

You may be facing things that don't look like they're ever going to change, but what God started, He's going to finish. It may not happen on your timetable. Instead of just asking God to get you out, being frustrated because it's taking longer than you hoped, why don't you do as Joseph did and ask God to come into that difficulty? "Lord, thank You that You're with me in this battle with cancer. You're with me in this struggle with the addiction. You're with me in the loss, in the divorce, in this trouble at work." When you ask Him to come in, you're going to feel His presence in a new way.

Who's in Your Boat?

In Mark 4, Jesus said to His disciples, "Let us cross to the other side of the lake." They all got in the boat, and as they were sailing, a huge storm arose. The waves were crashing over the boat, the winds so strong. The disciples started panicking, thinking they were about to die. Jesus was in the back of the boat asleep. They ran as fast as they could

> *When Jesus said "we're" going to the other side, you would think they would be confident.*

and said, "Jesus, wake up. Don't you care that we're about to die?" Jesus got up and spoke to the storm, "Peace, be still!" and everything calmed down. These disciples had seen Jesus perform great miracles, heal lepers, and raise a little boy from the dead. When Jesus said "we're" going to the other side, you would think they would be confident. "We have nothing to worry about, because the Son of God is in our boat. He just said we're going across." Even though Jesus was with them, they panicked. They didn't realize that the wind and waves couldn't stop the God who created the winds and waves. They had no reason to be afraid. Jesus was in the storm with them.

I wonder if you're doing like them. You're worried about something even though God is in your boat. He's already promised you that He will restore health to you, that you will lend and not borrow, that you and your house will serve the Lord. But maybe the medical report is not good, you had a setback in your finances, your family member is off course. It's easy to live upset and worried. Can I encourage you that the Most High God is in your boat? The winds can't stop you. The sickness, the injustice, and the people trying to discredit you can't keep you from your purpose.

You might as well relax, because everything is going to be fine for you. The waves may be big, the winds strong, but you have an advantage—the God who controls the universe is right there with you. Start thanking Him that He's fighting your battles. Start shining where you are, being your best despite the difficulties. Don't wait until it changes. You have to invite God in before He'll bring you out. If you do as those three Hebrew teenagers did, I believe and declare that the fire is not going to burn you, and you're about to see the fourth man is with you. You are going to see unusual things happen—unusual favor, unusual increase, promotion, healing, strength, and breakthroughs.

CHAPTER THREE

Victory Begins in the Dark

The book of Genesis begins by telling how God created every-thing. It's interesting that it says, "The evening and the morning were the first day." You would think it would be the reverse, that "the morning and the evening were the first day," but God starts the day in the dark. At twelve a.m., nothing looks any different. If you didn't have a watch, you wouldn't know you've entered a new day. It's still dark outside. It looks the same as it did at nine o'clock, at ten o'clock, at eleven o'clock. There's no sign that something has changed. But when the clock strikes midnight, in that one second, with nothing looking any different, it goes from p.m. to a.m. It's still dark, but it's a new day.

It would make more sense if God started the day when the sun came up and it was light. At six or seven o'clock in the morning, when the dawn breaks, the light comes, it's obvious that it's a new day. We can see it, and things have changed. We hear the birds start chirping. The sun comes over the horizon. We have all this evidence that we've entered a new day. But God chose to start the day in the dark on purpose.

It's symbolic of how He does things in our lives. He gives us the promise that says we've come into a new day—that He's restoring health to us, that we're going to lend and not borrow, that our child is going to get back on course. We believe, we pray, and we stand on that promise, but nothing is changing. Nothing looks any different, nothing feels any different. It's still dark outside. "Joel, my back's still hurting. My business hasn't grown. My health hasn't improved." This is what faith is all about. You can't see it, but you have to know that you've passed midnight. You've gone from p.m. to a.m. Yes, it's still dark outside, and nothing has changed, but the sun is on its way up. Healing is on the horizon, along with promotion, freedom, and the right people. It's just a matter of time before you see the light breaking forth.

Who Can Keep the Sun from Rising?

Don't get discouraged by the dark. The dark doesn't mean that nothing has changed. The dark is not a sign that God is not working, that He didn't hear your prayer. Thoughts will tell you, *You would have seen something by now. You would feel a little better. One of those companies would have called you back. That addiction wouldn't be this strong.* You have to walk by faith and not by sight.

> *It's a new day. You may not see any sign of it; that's okay, because victory begins in the dark.*

If you walk by sight, you'll talk yourself out of it, because 11:30 p.m. doesn't look any different than midnight. Everything you can see, feel, touch, and smell looks just the same. There's no evidence that it's a new day. But the psalmist says, "The moment you pray, the tide of the battle turns." You can't see it, but when you prayed, you left the p.m. and you came into a.m. It's a new day. You may not see any sign of it; that's okay, because victory begins in the dark.

We all go through times when we don't think things are going to work out, seasons where nothing is changing. We're being our best, but the business isn't growing. We're standing in faith, but our health is not improving. It's tempting to think that God has forgotten about us and we're always going to have this obstacle. But the fact is, light is on the way. What God promised is en route. You may have struggled in an area for a long time. You've been believing for things to change in your marriage, your finances, or with an addiction, but it seems permanent, as though it's never going to improve. God is saying, "You've already entered a new day. You've already passed midnight. You can't see it yet, but victory is on the way."

Now instead of complaining about the dark, have a new perspective. The dark means the sun is on the way up. The promise is about to come forth. Who can stop the sun from rising each morning? Who can keep the light from breaking forth over the horizon? All the forces of darkness cannot stop what God has ordained for you. They cannot keep what He promised from coming to pass. In the face of that

> *The dark means the sun is on the way up. The promise is about to come forth.*

darkness, when you don't see any light, get in agreement with God and say, "Father, thank You that it's a new day. It may still be dark out, but I don't go by what I see, I go by what I know. I know I've

passed midnight, which means my healing is coming, my breakthrough is coming, my abundance is coming, my victory is coming." When you realize God starts with darkness to bring about
new things in your life, you won't get discouraged by the darkness.
You'll thank Him in the midst of the darkness, and you'll praise
Him despite what's trying to stop you.

The Moment You Begin to Praise

This is what the apostle Paul and Silas did in Acts 16. They had
been put in prison for sharing their faith in the city of Philippi. The
owners of a female slave who made them rich through her fortune-
telling were angry with them after Paul set her free from that spirit,
and the owners accused them of causing a disturbance. They were
bound in the deepest part of the dungeon to make sure they couldn't
escape. But God won't let you get in a problem that He can't get you
out of. If that difficulty you're facing was going to stop your destiny,
God wouldn't have allowed it. It may seem too big for you, that you
could never overcome it, but it's not too big for our God. He already
has the solution. That trouble can't keep you from your purpose.
That setback in your finances, the anxiety, or the depression is not
permanent. It may be dark now. You've had some bad breaks, or you
brought trouble on yourself. Now you think you're stuck, but no,
get ready. God is not through with you. What He ordained for your
life will come to pass. That difficulty is a setup for Him to show out
in your life. He's going to do something unusual, something out of
the ordinary that will thrust you into your purpose, something that
will suddenly change things in your favor.

Paul and Silas had their feet securely chained in wooden stocks, with guards standing outside the prison doors. It looked as though they would be put away and we'd never hear from them again. All the odds were against them. But people don't have the final say. What you're up against may be bigger, more powerful, and more influential, but you and God are a majority. His being for

> *What you're up against may be bigger, more powerful, and more influential, but you and God are a majority.*

you is more than the world being against you. There's not an obstacle He can't move. There's not a sickness He can't heal nor an addiction He can't free you from. Sitting in the dungeon, having been falsely accused and beaten with rods, Paul and Silas could have been depressed. They could have said, "God, it's not fair. Why did this happen? We were doing what You wanted us to do." But the Scripture says, "At midnight they were praying and singing praises and giving thanks to God." It's interesting that we're told what time this happened. We're not given the time of most of the other miracles we read about in Scripture. That detail isn't recorded. But God had the writer tell us the time here because midnight means it was a new day.

As Paul and Silas were singing praises, suddenly there was a great earthquake. The prison doors flew open, the chains fell off their feet, and they walked out as free men. It's not a coincidence that this all happened at midnight. They may have been singing at ten o'clock in the evening, but nothing happened. They may have been thanking God at eleven o'clock, but nothing happened. They may have been praising some more at eleven thirty, still nothing. But when the clock struck midnight, when that new day started, suddenly things changed. God was showing us that it may be dark all around you, and you don't see a way out, but when you come into that new day, when you cross from p.m. to a.m., things suddenly shift. Sometimes you see it all at once, as Paul and Silas did, and other times you see it later. But the moment you begin to praise, things change in your favor. There may be a period of darkness when it doesn't look like anything is happening, but if you do as they did and just keep thanking God that He's fighting your battles, thanking Him that He's making a way where you don't see a way, then you're going to come into these times where God will suddenly show out in your life. He'll make things happen that you couldn't make happen.

You've Passed Midnight

You may have areas in your life where it feels dark right now. If nothing is changing, that's a test. Will you praise Him in the dark? Will you thank Him that what He promised is on the way? Will you talk as if it's going to turn around? Will you believe that healing is coming even though the medical report isn't improving? Don't go by what you feel. Your feelings don't always tell you the truth. Your emotions will try to convince you that it's never going to work out. Your mind will tell you all the reasons it's not going to happen. "Look how big the obstacles are." Walk by faith and say, "Father, thank You that I've come into my midnight, that it's a new day. It may still be dark, but I know that You start the day in the dark. I know this means the light is on the way." Keep a song of praise in your heart.

"Well, Joel, I've been doing this a long time. I don't understand why nothing is changing." God's timing is not our timing. Keep doing the right thing. You're in a new day. You've passed midnight. It may be three in the morning, and you have a few more hours before the sun comes up, so to speak. I've learned that the longer it's taking, the better it's going to be. God is getting you prepared for the blessing He's already prepared for you. When it's taking a long time, that's because the

> *Don't be discouraged because it's been dark a long time—that's a sign that God is about to do something you've never seen.*

blessing is bigger than you can handle right now. He's getting you stronger, more mature, more confident. He's getting other people who are involved in place. He's doing a work in them. Don't be discouraged because it's been dark a long time—that's a sign that God is about to do something you've never seen. It's going to be bigger, more rewarding, and more fulfilling than you've imagined. Now keep praising Him in the dark, thanking Him in the dark, being good to others in the dark, giving and serving in the dark. When you do as Paul and Silas did, suddenly doors are going to open. Suddenly you're going to come into opportunity, the right people, healing, breakthroughs. It's going to catapult you ahead.

Light Is Coming

When my mother was diagnosed with terminal cancer in 1981, she had been in the hospital for twenty-one days. On a Monday evening, the doctors called my father in and said there was nothing more they could do for her. They gave her a few weeks to live. My father drove her home through the afternoon traffic. It felt like the longest drive of their lives. It was a very dark time. My mother could have been depressed and given up on life, but she knew God is a healer and that He has the final say. She and my father went to their bedroom, lay down on the floor, and prayed together. God says in Psalm 50, "Call upon Me in the day of trouble, and I will deliver you." A lot of times in our difficulties we call people, call friends, call relatives, call experts, and that's all fine, but make sure you call out to God. Ask Him to help you. He created the universe. He flung stars into space. He has all power. You don't have to beg Him, and you don't have to plead with Him. He's longing to be good to you. The Scripture says, "It is your Father's good pleasure to give you the kingdom." Just ask in faith for what He's already promised.

One of the most powerful things you can do is take God's Word to Him. Remind Him of what He said. "Father, You said You would restore health to me. I'm asking for Your healing. I'm asking You to do what medicine cannot do." Take His Word and pray bold prayers. "Father, You said my children will be mighty in the land. I'm asking you to free my son from the addiction, to take away the wrong friends, to help him fulfill his destiny." Or, "Father, You said I would prosper and be in health, that I will lend and not borrow. You said that You are Jehovah-Jireh, the Lord my provider. So, Lord, I'm asking You to supply all my needs. Make rivers in the desert and give me overflow so I can be a bigger blessing."

> *One of the most powerful things you can do is take God's Word to Him. Remind Him of what He said.*

On December 11, 1981, my mother and father prayed and asked God to heal her from that cancer and give her more years. My mother believed that on that day she received her healing, that she came into her midnight. She went from p.m. to a.m., but nothing looked any different. She was still very frail, her skin was still yellow, and she only weighed eighty-nine pounds. I never heard her complain, and she never talked defeat. She would go through the house quoting Scripture: "I will live and not die and declare the works of the Lord." It was still dark. The medical report hadn't changed. Month after month, there was no sign of improvement.

All of my mother's senses said, "It's not going to work out." She didn't look good, and she didn't feel well. Her emotions and her thoughts said she wasn't going to make it, but she wasn't moved by that. She kept thanking God, walking by faith and not by sight. Sight said, "It's dark. Nothing has changed. You'll never get well." But faith said, "I've entered a new day. It's dark now, but light is coming. It's just a matter of time before healing breaks over the horizon." It didn't happen suddenly as it did for Paul and Silas, but over time, little by little she started getting better and better. Her skin color returned to normal, she regained her weight, and she got her strength back. Forty years later, she's perfectly healthy and whole. No cancer in her body. God has the final say.

Don't Be Moved by What You See

It may be dark in your life right now, but don't let the dark fool you. The dark is not a sign that you're never going to get well, it's not a sign that your child is never going to do right, and it's not a sign your business is never going to make it. It may have been meant to stop you, the enemy sent it to keep you from your destiny, but the good is that God has overruled that scheme. He's thwarting the plans of the enemy. That darkness is not going to last. The depression is not permanent. The addiction, the sickness, or the trouble at work is not how your story ends. You've gone from p.m. to a.m. It's a new day. The sun is about to break forth. Healing is in your future, abundance is in your future, good relationships are in your future, and victory is in your future.

Instead of complaining and being discouraged by the dark, have a new perspective. The dark means light is coming. Now do your part and start praising Him in the dark. Start thanking Him that things are changing in your favor. Don't be moved by what you see. Eleven thirty at night doesn't look any different than midnight, but midnight is a new day. God is saying, "The clock has ticked in your favor." You've passed midnight. Things may not look any different yet, but don't worry, for light is on the way. The sun has never once not come up. God has never once not made good on His promises. It may not happen on our timetable or in the way we thought, but I can assure you the sun is going to come up in your life. You wouldn't be alive if God didn't have something amazing in your future.

"Well, Joel, it sure feels like midnight." Midnight is a good thing. God always starts in the dark. That's a sign He's about to birth something new, something big, something unusual. If He started in the light, it wouldn't take any faith. If we could see how it was going to happen and we had all the resources, the

> *Midnight is a good thing. God always starts in the dark.*

connections, and the solution, we wouldn't have to depend on Him. The time to show what you're made of is when it's dark and you don't see anything changing. Thoughts will tell you, *You'll never get out of debt, never meet the right person, and never accomplish your dream.* Instead of getting depressed, the right attitude is: *Yes, it's still dark. Yes, I don't see anything changing, but I'm not worried. I know it's after midnight, and the light is coming.* God is faithful. What He promised, He's going to bring to pass.

Know That Your Redeemer Lives

In the Scripture, Job went through a dark time. Everything was going great, life was good, then the bottom fell out. He lost his health, lost his family, and lost his business. It didn't seem fair. The Scripture says, "Job was the most righteous man of his day." You wouldn't think he'd ever have a dark season, that he wouldn't have to deal with disappointments or bad breaks, but life happens to us all. Rain falls on the just and the unjust. The difference with the just, with people like you who honor God, is that God promises to take what was meant for your harm and turn it for your good. There may be dark seasons, but if you stay in faith and don't get bitter, God won't just bring you out, He'll bring you out better than you were before. He'll make the enemy pay for bringing the trouble.

God said to Satan, "Have you seen my servant Job? There's no one like him in all the land. He's blameless. He's a man of integrity. He has a spirit of excellence." I love the fact that God was bragging on Job. If you could hear what God is saying about you, you would be amazed. We think God is focused on all our faults and short-comings, but God sees all the good things in you. He sees your

> *Just because you're having difficulty doesn't mean you've done something wrong. We all go through tests, seasons we don't understand.*

heart to help others. He sees your sincerity, your kindness, and your courage. I can hear Him telling the angels, "Have you seen my son Jim? He's really amazing. Have you seen my daughter Rachel? There's no one like her." God is proud of you. He made you in His own image, and He calls you a masterpiece. Just because you're having difficulty doesn't mean you've done something wrong. We all go through tests, seasons we don't understand. What I want you to see is that the darkness is not permanent. At some point you're going to go from p.m. to a.m. God is going to shift things. You're going to come out promoted, increased, at a new level of your destiny.

When Job lost everything, he was very discouraged. He sat down among the ashes and put on sackcloth. He went through phases of being upset, bitter, confused, and frustrated. God knows we're human. We feel things. There may be times when you feel those emotions, which is okay. Just don't stay there. Job eventually got up and stepped out of the ashes. It was still dark, nothing had changed, but he said, "I know that God has granted me favor." He was saying, "I know I've entered a new day. I know I've gone from p.m. to a.m. I know this darkness is not permanent." A few chapters later, still in the middle of all the difficulty, still as dark as ever, with nothing having changed, Job said, "I know my Redeemer lives." He was saying, "God is still on the throne. He has the final say. I'm not going to drag around sour over what I've lost. I'm getting ready for the new things God has in store."

In Chapter 8 of the book of Job, a friend came along to encourage him and said, "Job, God will yet fill your mouth with laughter and your lips with shouts of joy." He was saying to Job what God is saying to us: "Don't let a dark season fool you. Don't let a pandemic, don't let a sickness, don't let a breakup cause you to live defeated. You're going to laugh again, you're going to love again, and you're going to dream again. You're going to build again, you're going to lead again, and you're going to flourish again."

A Sign That Double Is Coming

I've heard it asked, "What if the darkness you're going through is not the darkness of the tomb but the darkness of the womb? What if the darkness is what precedes God birthing something amazing in your life?" Have a new perspective. You're not in the darkness of the tomb, you're in the darkness of the womb. God is about to do something that you haven't seen. You're going to discover talent that you didn't know you had. That person who left and broke your heart didn't stop your destiny. You're about to meet someone better than you ever imagined. That dark time is not wasted. God is using it to birth something that you could never have experienced without it.

> *What if the darkness you're going through is not the darkness of the tomb but the darkness of the womb?*

When my father went to be with the Lord, that was a dark time for me. But I can tell you now that I wasn't in the darkness of the tomb, I was in the darkness of the womb. God birthed talent in me that I hadn't known was there. He took what I thought would be the darkest hour of my life and turned it into the brightest hour. The Scripture says, "God will turn your mourning into dancing. He will take away your sadness and clothe you with joy." I believe there's some sadness that's about to be taken away from you. That darkness is about to lift off you. You're going to be clothed with joy. You're going to be happy, fulfilled, and vibrant with a fresh vision, a fresh passion. You won't just come out okay and say, "I made it through." That mourning is about to be turned to dancing. God is going to make up for the sadness. He's going to pay you back for the sorrow, the hurt, the injustice. Now get your hopes up. As Job did, keep thanking Him that He's granted you favor. Keep declaring, "My Redeemer lives."

Job went through the dark season, but that's not where he ended. The Scripture says, "God restored back to Job twice what he had before. He was more blessed in the second part of his life than he was the first." Yes, it was dark, but when the sun rose, he came out with double. Don't believe the lies that the darkness is permanent, that it's never going to change. The darkness is a sign that double is coming. The sun is going to rise in your life again. You're going to see the goodness of God in ways that you've never seen. He's breathing in your direction right now. In the unseen realm, things are changing in your favor. Forces of darkness are being pushed out. The right breaks are headed your way. He's going to make things happen that you couldn't make happen. You're going to know it was the hand of God.

When we talk about this dark season in Job's life, we think it must have lasted fifty years, that was such a tough time. But some commentators believe that difficulty was only a nine-month period. It wasn't years and years. What you're dealing with is not going to last as long as it looks. It's not going to hinder you for the rest of your life. The sun is going to come up sooner than you think. You're already way past midnight. Daybreak is about to happen. Light is about to break forth on the horizon. Get ready for favor, get ready for breakthroughs, get ready for double. You're not in the darkness of the tomb, you're in the darkness of the womb. God is about to birth something out of this that thrusts you to a new level. My challenge is, trust Him in the dark. You may not see anything improving, but that's okay. Walk by faith and not by sight. If you do this, I believe and declare God is going to turn your mourning into dancing, your sadness into joy. As Job did, you're going to come out restored, promoted, healthy, free, and stronger than you were before.

CHAPTER FOUR

The Fight for Your Future

We all have things come against us in life, whether it's people who aren't fair, a sickness that won't seem to go away, or a setback in our finances. Sometimes it wasn't any fault of our own. Maybe we were born into difficulties, with parents who weren't around. Depression, addiction, and mediocrity just keep getting passed down through the generations. We wonder, *Why am I having this opposition? Why was I raised in an unhealthy environment? Why did this company let me go after all these years?* It's because there's something in you that the enemy is trying to stop. Those bad breaks weren't random, and you weren't just unlucky. Those were strategic attacks. If the enemy wasn't threatened by you, he wouldn't be trying to hold you back. If he didn't know there was greatness in you, he wouldn't waste his time bringing those challenges. When you gave your life to Christ, God marked you. He said, "You're mine." He put a crown of favor on your head. That's all great, but the challenge is that you became a target to the enemy. He knows you are destined to take new ground. He knows God has favored you to leave your mark, so he's going to work overtime to try to stop you.

Many times the enemy knows who we are even before we realize who we are.

When David was a teenager working out in the shepherds' fields, taking care of his father's sheep, he seemed as ordinary as can be. He wasn't incredibly handsome. He didn't come from wealth or influence. They were a low-income family. Nothing stood out about him. Why did David's father leave him out in the shepherds' fields when Samuel came to anoint one of his sons as the next king? It was no big deal to bring him in. Why did his father look down on him and disrespect him? Later, when David carried a supply of food to his brothers who were serving in the army, he had to travel a couple of days. He was being kind to them. Why did his oldest brother make fun of him and belittle him in front of other soldiers? Why was he jealous? David wasn't intimidating. He didn't seem like he was any threat to them. But the enemy can see things in you that you may not see. David saw himself as ordinary, but the enemy knew he could become a giant killer. He knew David would be a history maker if he wasn't stopped. That's why he came against David so strongly.

Many of the challenges you've faced—the things that didn't seem fair, the obstacles that came out of nowhere, the people who turned on you—are because there's a giant killer in you, there's a history maker inside. You may not see it yet, but the enemy can see that there's greatness in you. Have a new perspective. Those difficulties are a sign that something amazing is in your future.

> *You may not see it yet, but the enemy can see that there's greatness in you.*

It's Not Your Battle

In Mark 5, there was a man who was possessed with evil spirits. It had gotten so bad that no one could control him. He lived in the region of the Gerasenes, a Gentile region to the east of the Sea of Galilee and the Jordan River, in a place among the tombs, in a graveyard, a desolate place. They had tried to chain him up, but he was so strong he would break the chains. All through the day and night he would wander through the tombs wearing no clothes, screaming and cutting himself. It didn't seem like this man had a chance—he was mentally deranged, his family had given up on him, and society had written him off. But I can imagine that on some nights there were moments of sanity. All of a sudden he would think, *God, please help me. I want to see my children. I want to go home. Why am I so tormented?* I can see his little boy praying for him, and his wife weeping for him, feeling so discouraged. I'm sure that his parents were heartbroken, knowing their son was so deranged. It looked as though that was his destiny.

People had given up on him, but God doesn't give up on any of us. Nobody is too far gone. Don't write off your child, don't write off your neighbor, and don't write off your cousin. It may seem as though they're too bad, too addicted, too depressed, too sick, or too off course. The enemy wouldn't be fighting them this hard if he didn't know there was something amazing inside them.

Jesus was on the opposite side of the Sea of Galilee from where this man was, teaching the people on the shore. At the end of the day, instead of going to rest where He normally did, He told His disciples He wanted to get in the boat and travel to the other side of the lake. But in the middle of the night, a huge storm arose. The waves started crashing over the boat, filling it with water. The winds were so strong it seemed as though the boat was about to break apart. Jesus was in the back of the boat sleeping. The disciples frantically ran to him and said, "Jesus, wake up! We're about to die." Jesus stood up and spoke to the storm, "Peace, be still!" Suddenly the winds and waves stopped. Everything was perfectly calm.

That morning as they arrived at the shore, Jesus was getting out of the boat when this deranged man came running up to Him, fell on his knees, and let out a loud scream. Jesus told the demons to come out, and instantly the man was healed. When the local people heard about it and came to see what had happened, the Scripture says, "The people saw the man sitting there, clothed and in his right mind." What's interesting is that when Jesus was on the boat, headed toward that man, the huge storm that arose wasn't random. That wasn't just an act of nature, just a coincidence. That was the enemy trying to stop Jesus from getting to this man. You would think the enemy would have been satisfied that the man was possessed, out of his mind, and cutting himself. Surely this man was no threat. He could never do anything great. But, no, the enemy knew that despite all he had done to the man, despite all the turmoil, all the confusion, and all the cutting, this man still had greatness in him. He still had a purpose to fulfill and dreams to accomplish. When the enemy saw Jesus crossing the lake, he thought, *I have to stop Him. I have to keep Him from reaching that shore.*

There is a fight for your future, but what I want you to see is that it's not your battle. God is fighting for you. The enemy may send a storm of opposition that looks too big, but don't worry. God con-

> *There's no storm so strong that He can't calm it, no giant so big that He can't defeat it, and no fire so hot that He can't step into it and bring you out.*

trols the winds. He overrides every negative force. Those winds that are trying to keep you from your destiny, God is speaking to them right now. Breakthroughs are coming, healing is coming, and freedom is coming. Things may look as though they could never turn around. The storm is darker than ever. On your own, you're done, but you're not on your own. Get ready, because peace is coming, favor is coming, victory is coming. As this man did, you're going to see God override what's trying to stop you. There's no storm so strong that He can't calm it, no giant so big that He can't defeat it, and no fire so hot that He can't step into it and bring you out. There's no lion so hungry that He can't close its mouth, and no Pharaoh so powerful that He can't change his mind.

The Enemy Will Not Triumph over You

This man who was deranged didn't know that Jesus had spoken to the winds. He didn't know there was a huge storm or that Jesus had gone to great lengths to get to him. He just saw Jesus show up on the shore. You don't know all the storms the enemy has sent to try to keep God from getting to you. You don't know how many times God has said, "Peace, be still! That's my son, that's my daughter. They're going to fulfill their destiny. I'm going to break their chains. I'm releasing freedom, healing, and abundance to move them into their purpose." God has been fighting for you, pushing through forces of darkness, calming the storms, and crossing lakes just to get to you through your whole life.

Some of these battles started when you were a small child. The enemy knew way back then that God had a calling upon your life. He could see the favor and anointing on you. He could see you were destined for greatness, so through things that you

> *God has been fighting for you, pushing through forces of darkness, calming the storms, and crossing lakes just to get to you through your whole life.*

had no control over, he's worked overtime trying to stop your destiny. As a two-year-old, my father was walking by a fire and fell in it when nobody was around. He should have been killed, but his brother came out of nowhere and pulled him out. My father couldn't have saved himself. That was God fighting for him. The enemy sent the storm, but God said, "Peace, be still! I have the final say." The enemy can't end your life or stop your destiny.

David said in Psalm 30, "I praise You, O Lord, for You refused to let my enemies triumph over me." Why did that fire not take my father out? God refused to let the enemy triumph. Why did that accident not harm you? God refused to let it harm you. Why did that cancer not defeat you, or why did that unhealthy childhood not stop you, or why hasn't that addiction finished you off? Because God's purpose is more powerful than the enemy's plan. Forces of darkness cannot stop what God has ordained for you. If you only knew all the things God has refused to let happen to you.

You may have had bad breaks, things that aren't fair, but just the fact that you're still here is a sign that God's favor is on you. He's been pushing back forces of darkness your whole life.

There may be obstacles trying to stop you now. If you wonder why it's happening, it's because there's greatness in you. The enemy doesn't come against people who don't have anything. If you weren't a threat, he'd leave you alone. In one sense you can take it as a compliment. "Yes, I have some big obstacles, but I know it's because I have a big destiny. I didn't have a good childhood. I went through a breakup that wasn't fair, but I'm still standing. God refused to let it finish me off." The enemy wouldn't have wasted so much time and energy on you if there wasn't something amazing in front of you. Now do your part and stay in faith. Don't get bitter. Don't go around complaining about what you didn't get or what didn't work out. God is still working. He's a God of justice. He'll make up for what was unfair. He'll pay you back for the wrongs that were done.

> *The enemy wouldn't have wasted so much time and energy on you if there wasn't something amazing in front of you.*

Way back when my father was a little boy, the enemy knew that there were seeds of greatness in him. He recognized that my father had the potential to be the first one in the family to come to know the Lord. He knew that my father was a threat to break the cycle of poverty that had limited our family for generations. He recognized the heart of a pastor in my father who could start Lakewood,

> *When you have a big future, the enemy is not going to roll out the red carpet and let you fulfill it.*

make an impact on the world, and leave children and grandchildren who would continue it. No wonder the enemy tried to take his life in the fire. No wonder family members told him that all he knew how to do was pick cotton, and he couldn't become a minister. No wonder he went through a painful breakup in a relationship that could have ended his ministry. No wonder he felt he had to resign from one pastorate because his message of faith and victory didn't fit in. When you have a big future, the enemy is not going to roll out the red carpet and let you fulfill it. The apostle Paul said, "A wide door of opportunity is open for me, and there are many adversaries." The many adversaries are not because God has forgotten about you or because you got shortchanged. It's because of the wide doors that are about to open. It's because of the favor that's in your future.

When you look back over your life, you can see things that came against you. Some of those things you had nothing to do with. Some were unfair, times when you were left out or mischaracterized and made to look bad. Other times you tried to step up to a new level, you tried to set a new standard, but opposition came out of the woodwork, things you had never faced. There are forces that don't want you to take new ground. When the enemy sees you start to make progress, he'll send the storm, the waves, the winds. That's when God will step up and say, "Peace, be still!" The storm can't stop our God. He controls the winds. What's come against you is not a sign that you're stuck; it's a sign that promotion is coming. The storm is a sign that God is close to the shore. You're about to see things change in your favor.

Adversity Is a Sign of Greatness

In the Scripture, when Moses was born, Pharaoh had put out a decree that all the male Hebrew babies were to be killed. Pharaoh was afraid the Israelites were getting too strong, and they could eventually overthrow the Egyptians. At the time of Moses' birth, it says that Moses' mother "saw there was something special about him," something that said there was greatness in him. What she saw did not go unnoticed by the enemy. This child was a threat to the enemy's plans to keep the Israelites in slavery. It's not a coincidence that he was born into adversity, born with forces against him. It wasn't anything he had done. It wasn't because of poor choices he had made. But from his birth, the enemy was trying to stop him. Moses' mother hid him in the house for three months, until he was too big. She thought he would be found and killed. So she put him in a basket coated with tar and pitch and put it among the reeds along the Nile River. It just so happened that when Pharaoh's daughter went out to bathe in the river, she heard the cries coming from the basket, opened it, and couldn't believe it. She fell in love with this baby.

What's interesting is that she knew he was a Hebrew baby, and she knew he wasn't supposed to live. Her father was the one who made the decree. But for some reason she and Pharaoh decided it was okay for her to keep the baby and raise him as her own. When God is fighting your battles, things will happen that don't make sense. When He says, "Peace, be still!" storms that look impossible will calm down.

Maybe you were raised in an environment that wasn't healthy.

You have a good reason to be sour and think you can't do anything great. You've been through too much. How do you know you're not a Moses? How do you know that adversity wasn't a sign that greatness is in you? How do you know that wasn't the enemy trying to push you

> *How do you know you're not a Moses?*

down to keep you from leaving your mark, but God was calming the storm, saying, "Peace, be still"? He didn't bring you through that because you're ordinary. If you didn't have something amazing in you, the enemy wouldn't have worked so hard to stop you. You have to step into your greatness. Quit believing the lies that you've had too many bad breaks, too much against you, that it's not fair. It doesn't have to be fair for God to do something awesome. In fact, when it's not fair, when you're the underdog, when life has tried to stop you, that's when God will show out the most.

It wasn't fair for David to be put down by his family, but that didn't stop him from taking the throne. It wasn't fair for Joseph to be thrown into a pit, sold into slavery, lied about, and put in prison. That didn't stop him from becoming the prime minister of Egypt. It wasn't fair for Moses to be born under a death threat, for his parents to have to hide him, or for him to not grow up in his own home. But that didn't stop him from delivering the Israelites. Who says it has to be fair for you to fulfill your destiny? No bad break, no injustice, no disappointment, and no person has cancelled God's plan for your life. Have a new perspective. The reason it's not fair is because there's something in you that the enemy doesn't want out. There's an assignment God has for you that the enemy is trying to stop. There's an anointing, an empowerment, a favor that he doesn't want you to see. The good news is, he doesn't have the final say.

It's Because You Have a Purpose

My sister Lisa was born with something like a form of cerebral palsy. The doctors told my parents she probably would never be able to walk or feed herself. During the first year, she couldn't lift her head and had no sucking reflexes. By the grace of God, she got better and defied the odds. Growing up, there were five of us kids, and all of us were very athletic and played sports except for Lisa. Having come through this birth injury, she couldn't do everything we did. When we were choosing teams to play kickball with our friends at the house, she would always be chosen last, right after my brother, Paul. It seemed as though it was one thing after another for Lisa. In her early twenties, she went through a breakup in a relationship that was very hurtful and wasn't fair.

In 1990, Lisa was working at the church, opening my father's mail when one of the packages exploded in her lap. It was a mail bomb. It blew part of her leg up and injured her stomach. She was rushed to the hospital and had to have surgery. The investigators said if the package would have been turned the long ways in her lap instead of sideways, it would have killed her instantly. It was a pipe bomb, and the nails shot out the side, away from her instead of into her.

> When the bomb exploded, God said, "Bomb, you can't finish her off. I have the final say."

Why did Lisa have all these things coming against her, starting when she was a little baby? The enemy knew there was something special in her, an anointing to teach, a gifting to lead, a favor to help build people. Every time the enemy tried to stop her, God stepped up and said, "Peace, be still!" When the bomb exploded, God said, "Bomb, you can't finish her off. I have the final say." God refused to let her enemies triumph. Lisa says, "I opened the bomb, but now I am the bomb."

What's come against you hasn't been random. Those are strategic attacks that come for one reason—because of what's in you. It's because you have purpose, destiny, and greatness. If you stay in faith and keep moving forward—not bitter because of what happened, not upset because of what you didn't get, not discouraged by the bad break—then at some point you're going to step into what the enemy didn't want you to see. You'll step into levels of favor, influence, and opportunity that you never dreamed. God is taking you where you can't go on your own.

When You Can't Fight for Yourself

A man I know grew up in a large family in Puerto Rico. He had seventeen brothers and sisters. His parents were heavily involved in witchcraft. When he was three years old, his mother was in a trance and declared over him that he was the son of Satan. He wasn't old enough to understand what was going on. Imagine having people speaking that over your life. It didn't seem fair. It looked as though he was at a disadvantage. But people don't have the final say. What you can't see is that behind the scenes, the Most High God is fighting for you. He overrules negative things that other people have spoken. At fifteen years old, he moved to New York with one of his brothers. Six months later, he was the leader of one of the most violent and feared street gangs. Fighting and stealing were a part of his everyday life. A year later, his best friend was stabbed and died in his arms.

Like the man who was deranged and cutting himself, it didn't look as though this young man had a future. If he survived, he would never amount to much. He was way off course. What he couldn't see was that God was crossing the lake to get to him. God was on His way to turn things around. When forces come against you that strongly, you can be assured it's because there's great purpose, great potential inside.

One night a minister came up to him on the street and invited him to a service he was having. This young man made fun of the minister and threatened to beat him up. But when you plant a seed, you never know when it's going to take root. The next night the young man and all his gang showed up at the service. They were planning to disrupt things and cause trouble, but as this young man heard about the love and forgiveness of God, he felt something he had never felt. At the end of the service, against all odds, he stood up and gave his life to Christ. Instantly, chains were broken off him. He felt a sense of purpose, a sense of destiny. He knew he was no longer the son of Satan; he was the son of the Most High God. When you can't fight for yourself, you have to know that God is fighting for you. He's bigger than any force that's trying to hold you back. He's bigger than negative words that were spoken over you. He's bigger than addictions, bigger than how you were raised, and bigger than any sickness. You wouldn't have those challenges if there wasn't greatness in you. Today, our friend Nicky Cruz goes all over the world telling people what God has done.

Nicky couldn't change things on his own. Being raised in that negative environment, he was at a disadvantage. The deranged man couldn't get free by himself either. When people could no longer help him, they sent him away. The good news is that you have someone fighting for you. God is pushing back forces of darkness. He's behind the scenes making things happen that you couldn't make happen. The Scripture says, "Stand still and you will see the deliverance of the Lord." You just keep doing the right

> *The good news is that you have someone fighting for you.*

thing, honoring God, and He'll take care of what's stopping you. He'll move people out of the way. He'll silence the opposition. He'll say, "Peace, be still!"

Something Bigger Is Coming

When I first started ministering back in 1999, it seemed as though everyone was for me. People were cheering me on, so encouraging. But after a few years, I began to face opposition—some people were not understanding me, critics were trying to discredit me. I thought, *Why is this coming against me? I'm just trying to keep the ministry going, just talking about the goodness of God. I'm not bothering anyone else.* I realize now that the enemy doesn't fight you for where you are; he fights you for where you're going. I thought I would always be at that same level. I was satisfied to keep the church going, but God had something bigger in me, things I couldn't see. The enemy wasn't fighting me for where I was, he was fighting me for the Compaq Center, he was fighting me for *Your Best Life Now* and my other books, for the SiriusXM channel, for the Nights of Hope.

You may be doing the right thing, but you have opposition, people trying to stop you, and unfair situations. It's because there's something in your future much bigger than you think. There's something that you can't see right now, but the enemy knows what's coming. He knows you're destined to be a giant killer, a history maker, and to affect generations to come. You're going to break the addiction, you're going to start the business, you're going to meet an amazing spouse. Now quit being discouraged by what's against you. If you weren't a threat, the enemy wouldn't be bothering you. It's because there's greatness in you. What you're up against may be bigger and stronger, and you can't change it on your own. Don't worry. In this fight for your future, it's not just up to you. God is fighting for you. He's crossing the lake right now, saying, "Peace, be still!" I believe and declare every chain that's held you back is being broken, and every storm is beginning to dissipate. The greatness in you is about to come out, with new levels of favor, influence, abundance, and purpose.

CHAPTER FIVE

Special Strength Is Coming

We all have times in life when we feel tired. We've been doing our best, standing strong, but it's been so long, nothing has changed, and now we're fatigued. We don't feel as though we have the strength to raise the children, the strength to fight the illness, the strength to pursue our dreams. I know a woman who has struggled with depression for years. She's always been so strong, so determined, but when I saw her recently, she was very discouraged. She said, "I don't have any fight left in me. I can't do it anymore." Sometimes we see that as a lack of faith. But God doesn't expect you to be strong all the time. He understands there will be times when we get weary, when we don't feel that we can go on. We've prayed, we've believed, but nothing has changed. Now the weight of what we're facing has left us exhausted. The good news is that God doesn't fault us for feeling weak. He doesn't say, "What's wrong with you? You need to have more faith."

The Scripture says, "When you are weak, He is strong." When you feel overwhelmed, like you can't go on, He comes in and gives you special strength. Strength that you didn't get on your own.

Strength to move forward when you should be stuck, strength to overcome that addiction, strength to outlast that opposition. You may feel weak and fatigued, but that is not your destiny. You're going to "run and not be weary, to walk and not faint." There's going to be a strength that's not natural but supernatural.

Strength to Outrun Some Chariots

This is what happened with the prophet Elijah in 1 Kings 18. There had been a drought in Samaria for three and a half years. Without rain, the Israelites were going to perish. There was no food, and no way to grow crops. Elijah climbed to the top of Mount Carmel and began to pray for rain, but nothing happened. He prayed again and again, had his assistant keep going out and checking the weather, looking for clouds forming over the sea, but still nothing. Finally, on the seventh time his assistant checked, he saw a small cloud starting to form in the sky. Elijah sent that assistant to tell King Ahab that he better get in his chariot and quickly leave because a huge downpour was coming. The Scripture says, "Then the Lord gave Elijah special strength, and he outran the king's chariot to Jezreel."

Jezreel wasn't just next door to Mount Carmel; it was a twenty-mile journey. A horse can run twice as fast as an average man, and a man can only sustain that top speed for a short distance. On top

> *You're going to overcome what looks impossible.*

of this, I'm sure that Elijah was tired, living in the midst of the severe famine, not having proper food. How could he outrun a chariot? That's not possible. God gave him special strength. You may look at what you're up against and think, *I don't have the strength. I don't have the stamina, the endurance, the fortitude. Maybe I did years ago, when I was at the top of my game, but now I'm tired.* No, get ready, for special strength is headed your way. When you have special strength, you're going to outrun some chariots. You're going to overcome what looks impossible. You're going to accomplish dreams that seem too far gone.

Jezreel was known as the city of chariots. It had a vast fleet of these powerful vehicles that could move swiftly into battle. They gave the people of Jezreel an incredible advantage. These chariots represented power and speed, the ability to dominate with force. Enemies knew not to come against Jezreel. It's significant that Elijah outran Ahab's chariot. I can imagine Elijah standing before King Ahab as he sat in his big, impressive, state-of-the-art chariot. Ahab had his drivers up front, and his staff in the back. Elijah looked up to King Ahab and said in effect, "You have a powerful army, and you command a vast fleet of chariots pulled by these fast, strong horses. I don't have your equipment, and I don't have your horses. I don't even have a chariot, but I'm not worried, because I don't need what you have. I'm going to outrun you to Jezreel."

I can hear Ahab laughing and saying, "What are you talking about, Elijah? These are the fastest horses of our day, these are the most skilled drivers, and this chariot just won the J.D. Power Chariot of the Year Award. You can't outrun me." However, the Scripture says that Elijah ran ahead of the chariot the whole way, for twenty miles. When Ahab got to the entrance of Jezreel, I can see Elijah sitting with his feet up, drinking a glass of tea, saying, "Ahab, what took you so long?" When God gives you special strength, you're going to accomplish things you never dreamed you could accomplish. You're going to overcome any opposition, even one that's more powerful and has more resources.

Strength for the Weary

You may not be up against a chariot, but when you look at the cancer, it seems so much bigger. The addiction, the trouble at work, the slowdown in your business—you don't see how you're going to make it. The difficulty is discouraging enough, but on top of that you're tired. You've been standing strong, but the famine, the lack of things changing, has worn you down. There's no way you can outrun this chariot. In your own strength you can't, but right now God is breathing special strength into you. Like Elijah, you're going to have the endurance, the stamina, the fortitude to do what you can't do on your own. You may think, *How can I raise my children and take care of my elderly parents at the same time? How can I make it through this treatment? How can I overcome this anxiety? I don't have the strength.* When you are weak, He is strong. Now get ready to outrun that chariot. God has not brought you this far to leave you.

The prophet Isaiah says, "God gives strength to the weary. He increases the power of the weak." You may be weary today, but the good news is that strength is coming. Maybe you feel weak and worn down by everything that's going on—the pandemic, the unrest, the uncertainty. God is saying, "I'm about to increase your power. I'm about to make you stronger." It's not something you have to muster up or make happen. It's the hand of God lifting you, empowering you, reenergizing you, causing you to outrun chariots. When God gives you special strength, that means strength to outlast, strength to try again, strength to step up to a new level.

When I look back over my life, I can see the times when God gave me special strength. When my father went to be with the Lord and I stepped up to pastor Lakewood, that should have overwhelmed me, caused me to lose my passion, and not be able to move forward. But I felt a

> *God is not going to let you miss your destiny.*

power rising up in me that I had never felt—a strength, a courage, a determination, a stamina. That wasn't just me being strong; that was God giving me special strength. God is not going to let you miss your destiny. He's not going to let you stay overwhelmed. You may feel that way at times, but that's not how your story ends. You're going to feel a strength that pushes you forward, a power to do what you couldn't do before.

A Second Wind Is Coming

When we were trying to acquire the Compaq Center, it was a three-year process. After we won the city council vote, a huge real estate company filed a lawsuit to try to keep us from moving in. They were the largest taxpayer in Texas. It was David versus Goliath. At first, I was passionate about it. I prayed, I believed, and I stood strong. But week after week went by and nothing changed, then month after month. One year passed, then two years. I started to get weary. Battle fatigue began to set in. It's not that we aren't strong, we just get tired of fighting. I thought, *They're so much bigger than us. They have so many more resources. They can drag this out for years.* God understands that we can get tired. He understands that life can wear us down. That's why He says, "I will give strength to the weary. I will increase the power of the weak."

Don't beat yourself up for feeling weary. Don't be down on yourself because you're not strong all the time. You're human. God's not faulting you. He's saying, "When you're weak, I'm going to step in. I'm going to make you strong. I'm going to give you power to outrun a chariot." "Well, Joel, I've been weary for a long time. I am exhausted. I don't see anything changing." Your time is coming. You wouldn't be reading this if special strength wasn't on the way. God hasn't forgotten about you. He sees what you're going through. He sees the lonely nights, the struggles, all those times you've gone the extra mile. He's about to increase your strength. The opposition may not have changed yet, but you're going to have a new passion, a new fire, to stand strong and outlast what's trying to stop you.

At one point when I didn't think I could go on, when it looked as though the lawsuit would never be resolved, suddenly it was as though God gave me a second wind. I had a determination that I didn't have before. It wasn't something I did; it was God giving strength to the weary. It wasn't long after that when the real estate company suddenly dropped the lawsuit and the building was ours. Like Elijah, we outran the chariot and defeated something much bigger, more powerful. How did that happen? God gave us special strength. The Scripture says, "Some trust in chariots, some trust in horses, but we trust in the name of the Lord our God." He is going to get you to where you're supposed to be.

Angels Are Going to Show Up

On the night before Jesus was to be crucified, He went into the Garden of Gethsemane to pray. He knew the pain and suffering He was about to face. Even though He is God, He is also human. Jesus could feel what we feel. He got tired. There were many times when He was weary, fatigued, and felt lonely. In that garden He was so discouraged

> *Jesus is the Son of God, yet He felt overwhelmed, as though He couldn't go on.*

and so overcome with emotion that His sweat became like great drops of blood. He told the disciples, "My soul is overwhelmed with sorrow." Jesus is the Son of God, yet He felt overwhelmed, as though He couldn't go on. You would think God would say, "Come on, You need to be stronger. You need to toughen up." But God understands that life can be overwhelming. There are times when we feel weary, tired, and distressed. It doesn't mean that we don't have enough faith. It doesn't mean we're not strong enough. When Jesus felt so overwhelmed, when it looked as if He wasn't going to fulfill His destiny, the Scripture says that God sent "an angel to strengthen Him."

You may be tired today—tired of believing for your dreams, tired of trying to make your marriage work, tired of raising your children. God sees what you're going through. He feels the weight of what you're carrying. He's not going to leave you there. He has angels coming your way to strengthen you, to encourage you, to lift you. Thoughts will try to convince you that you're not strong enough, that you need more faith. "Look at how tired and discouraged you are, letting this problem overcome you." Don't believe those lies. Jesus in His human body felt weak, He felt discouraged, and He didn't know if He could go on. God sees you being your best to raise your children, fighting the addiction, facing the illness. When you run out of strength, don't worry. Angels are coming. Help is on the way. You're going to feel strength that you didn't have, joy when you could be discouraged, and hope when you should be depressed. You're going to have the power to endure, the favor to overcome, and the determination to outlast. It's not because of your own efforts; it's the angels ministering to you.

Before Elijah outran the chariot, he had called down fire from Heaven and defeated four hundred and fifty false prophets who worshipped the god Baal. When King Ahab's wife, Jezebel, heard about it, she was furious. She sent word to Elijah saying, "May the gods strike me and even kill me if I haven't killed you by this time tomorrow." Elijah was so afraid that he took off running into the desert for a whole day. He ended up sitting under a tree, so exhausted and overwhelmed that he didn't want to live. He said, "God, I've had enough. I'm done. Take me home." He had just called down fire from Heaven, he had prayed on top of Mount Carmel for an outpouring of rain to end a famine, he had outrun a chariot, and he had seen God's goodness and favor, but he got tired. When we're tired, we can lose our perspective. Problems get magnified,

> *When we're tired, we can lose our perspective. Problems get magnified, the sickness looks bigger, and we think the trouble at work will never be resolved.*

the sickness looks bigger, and we think the trouble at work will never be resolved. We feel so overwhelmed that we can't go on. But the beauty of our God is that He understands what we're going through. He knows life can feel overwhelming. He knows it's difficult to get out of the Garden of Gethsemane on our own.

Elijah was sitting under that tree in the desert, so depressed that he did not want to live. This could have been the end of his story. But what happened? An angel showed up there, just as one did in the garden for Jesus. While Elijah was sleeping, this angel cooked him some food and brought him a jar of water. He woke Elijah up and told him to eat. Elijah looked up and saw freshly baked bread. He must have thought he was dreaming. He ate and went back to sleep. The Scripture says the angel woke him up a second time and said eat some more. Elijah ate the food, and it says he was strengthened by that food to make a forty-day journey. His whole attitude and perspective changed. He got his fire back. He realized that God was still on the throne and He was bigger than what he was facing. Elijah went on to fulfill his destiny.

What I want you to see is that when you are weak, God is going to strengthen you. When you can't go on, angels are going to show up and make things happen that you couldn't make happen. I love how the angel didn't just help Elijah find food and water, or just lead him to an animal or to a place where he could hunt. The angel not only brought the food to Elijah, but he cooked the food. God is not going to just help you get stronger, He's going to cook some food for you. He's going to bring blessings, increase, favor, and healing that He's already prepared. It's going to be easier than you thought, and it's going to happen sooner than you think.

Victory Breathed into Your Spirit

Martin Luther King Jr. told how in the height of the civil rights movement, when so much was coming against him, he felt overwhelmed one evening. He didn't know if he could go on. To make matters worse, in the middle of that night, the phone rang. When he answered, there was an angry voice telling him how he wasn't wanted in that town and how he was going to be harmed if he didn't leave. King was so distressed that he couldn't go back to sleep. He began to pace the floor in a state of exhaustion. He tried to think of a way to quietly bow out of leading the movement without appearing to be a coward. Feeling overwhelmed, with all his courage gone, he said, "God, I'm here taking a stand for what I believe is right, but I'm afraid. I'm at the end of my ability. I have nothing left to give. I cannot continue on." King said at that moment, he felt the hand of God, "the presence of the Divine as I had never experienced God before." God strengthened him, encouraged him, and breathed new life into his spirit. King said, "I was ready to face anything."

> *King said at that moment, he felt the hand of God, "the presence of the Divine as I had never experienced God before."*

What was that? A ministering angel. God is not going to let you give up. He's not going to let you get so discouraged that you can't become who you're created to be. You may feel that way at times when the task looks too big, the opposition too strong, the dream is taking too long. You don't have the strength. Don't worry. Angels are on the way. You're about to feel strength that you've never felt, power that you've never had. God is about to lift you. He's breathing victory into your spirit, encouragement and hope. It's not just strength but special strength. Strength that causes you to outrun a chariot, strength to overcome the sickness, strength to outlast what's trying to stop you, strength to accomplish what God put in your heart.

After Jesus was sentenced to be crucified at His trial, the custom was that the condemned person had to carry his own cross. Jesus was so exhausted. He had not slept the night before, and He'd gone through much suffering and pain during the trial. He did His best, He was as strong as He could be, but He fell down under the weight of His cross. God could have given Him the strength to carry it the whole way and not fall down. He could have given Him a second wind to finish the journey and not look weak. But God was sending this message: You don't have to be strong all the time. It's okay to feel overwhelmed. It's okay to say as Martin Luther King Jr. did: "God, I don't think I can do this." Sometimes the cross we're carrying gets heavy. We think, *This child is too hard to raise. I can't stay in this marriage. I can't deal with this sickness. I'm lonely. I'm hurting.* Voices will try to condemn you and say, "You don't have enough faith. You need to be stronger. God's not going to help you. You're too weak." Don't believe those lies. Even Jesus couldn't carry the weight of His own cross.

It's interesting that when Jesus fell down, God didn't leave Him there. He sent a man by the name of Simon to come across His path and carry the cross for Jesus. When you're down, when you're discouraged, God is not

> *When you're down, when you're discouraged, God is not going to leave you there.*

going to leave you there. He'll always have someone to help lift you back up, someone to encourage you, someone to help you carry the load that you can't carry. If it's not an angel, God will send a person. There will be a Simon there for you.

The Right People at the Right Time

On one occasion when Joshua and the Israelites were in a valley fighting the Amalekites, Moses stood on top of the hill and held his rod up in the air. As long as his rod was up, the Israelites were winning. When he put it down, the Amalekites would prevail. When the battle kept going longer and longer, Moses got tired. He couldn't hold his hands up that long. God didn't say, "Moses, you should be stronger. You should have more endurance, more stamina." No, God sent two men, Aaron and Hur, to help. They stood on each side of Moses and held his hands up for him. God has the right people who will be there to help hold up your hands. God knows we're going to get tired. He knows there will be times when we don't have the strength on our own to do what we need to do. He doesn't fault us or cancel our destiny. He sends the right people, an Aaron and Hur, to lift our hands.

God has the right people who will be there to help hold up your hands.

A few years after my father passed and I became pastor, everything was growing. We were seeing great favor and God's blessing, but at the same time there were people who didn't understand us. At one point it seemed as though things were coming against us from the left and the right. I had never had any opposition. I thought, *All we're doing is giving people hope and letting them know that God is good.* It didn't make sense to me why people would be against that. I was concerned about how it was going to work out. Thoughts told me that we weren't going to last, that these other voices were too strong. I was tempted to live worried, discouraged, and afraid.

One afternoon I had walked through the lobby of the church and was waiting for the elevator. When the doors opened, out stepped an older lady whom I'd known all my life but hadn't seen in years. She used to take care of me in the nursery, and I knew that she always prayed for me. When I was growing up, every time I saw her, she would smile and say, "Joel, you know I'm praying for you." I thought, *Yes, I know. You've told me four hundred times.* I gave her a hug, and she said, "Joel, I can't believe I ran into you. I was going to send you a note. When I was praying for you this morning, I heard God saying, 'Whatever you're worried about is all going to be fine. The opposition is not going to last.'" When she said that, it was like a weight lifted off me. I stepped into the elevator suddenly feeling strong, confident, and reenergized. If I had been there two minutes earlier, I would have missed her; two minutes later, and she would have been gone. God knows how to bring the Simons across your path at just the right time. People who will encourage you and help lift you back up will be there.

When You Feel Overwhelmed

Several months before Jesus was crucified, He went up a high mountain with Peter, James, and John. There Jesus' appearance changed. His face shone like the sun, and His clothes became dazzling white. It's known as the Mount of Transfiguration. Suddenly Moses and Elijah appeared before them and started talking with Jesus. It's interesting that those two men were chosen for this occasion. There were other great heroes of the faith, such as Abraham, David, and Joseph. Jesus was about to face all this hardship and suffering, to go through things that were very difficult, that could be overwhelming and exhausting. Perhaps Elijah was there because even though he had performed great miracles, even though he'd called down fire from Heaven and raised a little boy from the dead, at one point he was too exhausted to carry on, too weary to move forward, but then God sent an angel to strengthen him. I don't know what the conversation was, but maybe Elijah encouraged Jesus that God would give Him special strength to make it through, that angels would be there to minister to Him. Maybe Moses reminded Jesus how when he was too tired to hold up his hands, when he was fatigued and couldn't do it any longer, God sent people to hold up his hands for him, and that people would lift Him when He fell and help Him carry the weight of the cross.

Maybe God has you reading this to remind you that when you face these times of feeling fatigued and overwhelmed, when you don't have the strength to go on, that's okay. Jesus felt overwhelmed. Moses and Elijah didn't think they could go on. God is going to send angels to strengthen you, the right people are going to show up. God is not going to let you miss your destiny. He gives strength to the weary, not condemnation, not "Why aren't you stronger?" Take the pressure off. Even Jesus fell down under

> *Sometimes your cross is too heavy to carry by yourself.*

the weight of the cross. Sometimes your cross is too heavy to carry by yourself. Like Jesus, you may fall down, but God will always have a Simon there, someone to help you carry it.

Perhaps you don't feel you have the strength to move forward today, the strength to fight that illness, the strength to raise those children. Remember that when you are weak, He is strong. I believe that God is breathing special strength into you right now. That burden that's weighed you down is being lifted. This is a turning point. God is reenergizing you with fresh passion, fresh vision. You will run and not be weary, you will walk and not faint. Like Elijah, you're about to outrun some chariots. You're going to think, *Where did I get this energy, this power, this ability?* It's God giving you special strength. I believe and declare that you are strong, you are victorious, and you are well able. You're going to accomplish dreams bigger than you imagined, overcome obstacles that looked insurmountable, and reach the fullness of your destiny.

CHAPTER SIX

Who Do You Say You Are?

There are a lot of voices in life trying to define us, to tell us who we are. Sometimes they're uplifting, such as a parent telling us that we're talented and we can do great things. Other times they're negative: "You're not attractive. There's nothing special about you." Our own thoughts will try to label us, *You've made too many mistakes. You missed your chance.* When you listen to all these voices, it's easy to think, *Who's telling the truth? Who am I? Am I talented or am I ordinary? Am I strong and confident or am I weak and insecure? Do I have a bright future or have I blown it?* Here's the key: The only voice that matters is your voice. Who do you say you are? What you choose is what you will become. Instead of letting people define you, instead of letting circumstances label you, you need to go back to what God says about you. God says, "You can do all things through Christ. You're equipped and empowered." Other voices will tell you, "The problem is too big. You don't have what it takes." Who do you say you are? God says, "You have seeds of greatness. You are destined to leave your mark." Other voices will tell you, "You're just ordinary. You'll never do anything significant." You have the final choice. Who do you say you are?

The problem with some people is that they've chosen to listen to the wrong voices for so long that they don't know who they really are. They've let people label them, tell them what they're not and what they can't do. They've allowed circumstances, mistakes, and disappointments to define them, and now they've lost their passion. If you let these

> *The only One who knows who you really are is your Creator. He calls you a masterpiece.*

other voices play, it will keep you from your destiny. The only One who knows who you really are is your Creator. He calls you a masterpiece. He says you've been fearfully and wonderfully made. He says you will be mighty in the land. He says you are more than a conqueror—strong, confident, approved, and valuable. That's who you were created to be. When you say what God says about you, you activate what He put inside.

You can't say "I'm weak" and tap into the power. You can't say "I'll never get ahead" and tap into the abundance. You can't say "I'm not that talented" and tap into your greatness. Who do you say you are? Not who do other people say you are, or who does your family say you are, or who do your coworkers say you are? No disrespect, but you are not who people say you are; you are who God says you are. People can't always see what God put in you. They can't see the potential, the gifts, the greatness. If you let them put their limitations on you and convince you that you can't accomplish your dream, you'll never get out of debt or overcome that sickness. Then because you're letting them define you, what they're saying is going to come to pass. They may speak negative things, but it has no power if you don't let it get in you. Don't repeat the negative words that people have spoken over you.

You Are Who You Say You Are

In John 1, the Jewish leaders sent men out into the desert to find out who John the Baptist was. They had heard so much about him, and he had a large following. These leaders traveled from Jerusalem and asked John if he was the Christ. He told them no. They asked if he was Elijah. He said it again, "I'm not." They said, "Then tell us who you are, so we can give an answer to those who sent us. What do you say about yourself?" John could have answered many different ways. He could have told them about his background, his education, and his philosophy. But the Scripture says, "John replied in the words of Isaiah, 'I am a voice shouting in the wilderness, prepare the way for the Lord.'" He went back to what the Scripture said about him. He didn't say what he felt, he didn't say how he had been raised, and he didn't talk about what he was dealing with. He said what God said about him.

Imagine someone asking you, "Tell us who you say you are, so we can tell others?" What kind of answer would you have? "This illness has me worried, my back's been hurting, my business is slow, and these kids are getting on my nerves. I'm really discouraged." Zip that up. That is not who you are. Go back to the Scripture and say what God says about you. Your answer should be, "Tell them I'm strong, anointed, talented, favored, healthy, blessed, forgiven, and fearfully and wonderfully made."

We start off every church service saying, "I am what God says I am." I am not what I feel. I may feel weak, but God says I'm strong, so my report is that I am strong. When you say that, strength starts heading your way. You may not feel up to par. You're dealing with an illness, struggling with anxiety, fighting that depression. It's easy to wear the labels of sick, depressed, anxious, or defeated and to say, "That's just who I

> *Don't let that difficulty become your identity. Don't get in agreement with the negative.*

am." No, that's not who you are. That's what you're dealing with. You're not a sick person trying to get well. You're a well person fighting off sickness. Don't let that difficulty become your identity. Don't get in agreement with the negative. Go back to what your Creator says. God says He's restoring health to you. He says you will run and not be weary. He says weeping endures for a night, but joy is coming in the morning. What do you say about yourself? "I'm sick. I'm depressed." No, "I'm healthy. I'm whole. I'm energetic. I'm free. I'm happy. I'm victorious." If you start saying what God says about you instead of what you feel, you'll see things begin to turn around. Don't go through life wearing those negative labels.

I talked to a man who was so down on himself. He told me how he had made mistakes and didn't raise his children right. He was struggling with an addiction. He said, "I feel so unworthy. I don't deserve to be blessed." When you're down on yourself, it's not doing anything productive. Being against yourself is not going to help you move forward. The enemy is called "the accuser." He'll remind you of every mistake you've made, every time you've failed. He'd love for you to wear these labels: unworthy, washed-up, no future. I told this man what I'm telling you, that as long as you see yourself as unworthy, as undeserving, it's going to keep you where you are. Instead of wearing those labels, why don't you say what God says about you? "I'm forgiven. I'm redeemed. I'm restored. My past is over, and my future is bright."

Who do you say you are? Not who do your mistakes say you are, or who do your friends say you are, or who do the negative thoughts say you are? What you say overrides all the others. What you say gives it the right to come to pass. Now quit saying negative things about yourself. Don't say, "I'm so overweight. I'm so undisciplined. I'll never get out of this neighborhood. I'll never break this addiction." You're going to become what you believe. Why don't you start saying what God says about you? "I'm talented. I'm successful. I'm prosperous. I'm free. I'm valuable. I'm a masterpiece." What you say about yourself is going to become a reality. Who do you say you are? "I'm just average." You're going to be average, even though the truth is that God didn't make anyone average. Nobody has your fingerprints; nobody can do what you can do. But as long as you believe you're ordinary, you won't shine like you're supposed to shine.

You're No Ordinary Child

When Moses was born, the Scripture says, "He was no ordinary child." There was something special about him. As he grew up, he could sense his destiny was to deliver the Israelites out of slavery. He had good intentions, but he made a mistake and ended up having to flee to the desert. He spent forty years in hiding. I can imagine voices told him how he blew it, that he missed his chance. He could have worn the labels: failure, washed-up, too late. But deep down he could hear that still small voice telling him, "You are no ordinary child. This is not how your story ends. There is greatness in you." Just because you've made mistakes doesn't mean that stopped your destiny. What God started He's going to finish. What stops us is when we start wearing the negative labels, when we start believing that we're washed up, when we quit pursuing our dreams.

> *What stops us is when we start wearing the negative labels, when we start believing that we're washed up, when we quit pursuing our dreams.*

After forty years in the desert, God appeared to Moses and said, "Now it's your time to fulfill your destiny." He went on to deliver the Israelites, part the Red Sea, and do great things. I don't believe this would have happened if Moses had seen himself as a failure. "I've made too many mistakes." Instead he saw himself as no ordinary child. He kept the right image inside. When you were born, God said the same thing about you as He did Moses: "This is no ordinary child." God put greatness in you. He's destined you to leave your mark. You may have made mistakes, you may have obstacles, and it's taking longer than you thought, but that doesn't change what's in you. Now, the enemy will work overtime to try to steal your sense of value, your sense of worth. He knows that if he can distort your identity—who you are—and convince you that you're just average, that there's nothing special about you, then he can keep you from your greatness. I wonder what you could accomplish and how far God will take you if you will just live like you are no ordinary child. Not living arrogantly but knowing that God has placed greatness in you. You live knowing that there's a favor on your life that will take you where you can't go on your own, an anointing that will break every chain that's trying to hold you back, and a blessing that will cause you to stand out.

Who do you say you are? Not ordinary, not average, you are a child of the Most High God. You have royal blood flowing through your veins. You've been crowned with favor. What's trying to stop you doesn't have a chance. God being for you is more than the world being against you. That dream may seem too big, and for some people it is, but not for you. You're no ordinary child. That sickness should be the end, the medical report says you're done, but not for you. You're no ordinary child. That mistake you made should have stopped your destiny, it should have limited your future, but not for you. You are no ordinary child. God handpicked you. Before you could choose Him, He chose you. When He created you, God stepped back and said, "That was very good." God had created universes, flung stars into space, and made spectacular sunrises and magnificent mountain ranges, but He never said they were "very good." The only thing He said that about was you. Now don't go around thinking you're average, that you don't have much to offer. You are no ordinary child. You are a history maker. You are a world changer. You are destined to leave your mark.

"Joel, this sounds good, but I think you have the wrong person. There's nothing unusual about me. I'm not super-talented. I don't have a great personality. I don't come from an influential family." As long as you're discounting yourself, you're not going to see your greatness. Who do you say you are? If you say you're ordinary, just average, you're going to

> *As long as you're discounting yourself, you're not going to see your greatness.*

become that. I'm asking you to get in agreement with God. He says you are no ordinary child. It doesn't matter how you were raised. It's not dependent on how much education you have, how many connections you have, or what obstacles you're up against. When you believe what He says about you, doors will open that you never dreamed would open. God will take you further than you can imagine.

You Are Much More than You Think

The prophet Joel says, "Wake up the mighty men, wake up the mighty women." I want to wake up your greatness, wake up your dreams, wake up that business God put in you. I want to wake up that book, the movie, the song, the orphanage, or the ministry inside you. It may seem as though it's over your head, but you have to understand that you are no ordinary child. You're not average. You can accomplish much more than you think. You are stronger than you think. You are more anointed than you think. You are more favored than you think. You are more talented than you think. The dreams and gifts God put in you are much bigger than you think. If you're going to see the fullness of what's in you, you have to see yourself the right way. Who do you say you are? Don't you dare say, "I'm average. I'm ordinary." Get in agreement with God. "I am no ordinary child. I am highly favored. I am destined for greatness. I am surrounded with God's goodness." When you know you're an unusual child, you will see unusual favor, unusual healings, unusual doors open, and unusual breakthroughs.

When I stepped up to pastor the church, I felt ordinary and

unqualified. But you can't go by your feelings. I chose to believe what God says, that I am equipped and empowered. I had never ministered, and I didn't have the training or the experience. All the circumstances said I was average, that there was nothing special about me. But deep down I was bold enough to believe that I was no ordinary child. I didn't tell anyone, but I could feel the seeds of greatness. I could hear God whispering in the night that big doors were going to open. Victoria told me ten years before my father passed that one day, I would pastor the church. That seemed so odd to me. I thought, *Boy, I have her fooled. I can't get up in front of people.* I felt ordinary, but the Scripture says, "There is fire shut up in your bones." There is greatness shut up inside. As I stepped up, I discovered talent that I hadn't known was in me. There was a boldness and confidence that I'd never had before.

We would never have gotten the Compaq Center if I didn't believe that I was no ordinary child. When I heard it was coming available, I didn't think twice. I never thought about where we would get the funds or how it could happen. I just knew we were supposed to pursue it. When you know that you're no ordinary child, you'll go after dreams that seem too big. You'll pray bold prayers. You'll believe for things that most people think are impossible. There are Compaq Centers that have your name on them, dreams much bigger than you thought, businesses and ministries. How can it happen? You don't have the experience, the funding, or the connections. You are no ordinary child. There is a favor on your life that will catapult you ahead, a blessing that will cause

> *When you know that you're no ordinary child, you'll go after dreams that seem too big. You'll pray bold prayers.*

people to help you. God is not asking you to figure it out; He's just asking you to believe—not only believe in Him but believe in who He created you to be. Who do you say you are? If you're going to reach your destiny, if you're going to see your Compaq Centers, your dreams, and your healing, you have to know that you're not ordinary. There's something special about you. It is not because of who you are but because of whose you are. The Most High God breathed life into you. "Joel, I don't feel special." You don't have to feel it; you just have to believe it. If you believe it long enough, you'll not only feel it, but you'll see it.

I didn't feel special. I felt ordinary, but I chose to believe it by faith. Now every time I walk into our facility, I know I am no ordinary child. I know I couldn't have done this on my own, but the Creator of the universe favored me. I didn't think I could speak in front of people. I was too quiet, too reserved. Even now, every time I flip through the channels and see myself on television, I do a double take. I'm amazed at where God has taken me. I realize I am no ordinary child. No, I'm not bragging on me; I'm bragging on the greatness of our God. He wants to take you places that you've never dreamed. What He has planned for your future is bigger and more rewarding than you've ever imagined.

You Are a Mighty Hero

In Chapter One, we looked at the man named Gideon who was hiding in a winepress for fear of the Midianites. When an angel appeared to him and said, "Mighty hero, the Lord is with you," I can imagine Gideon looked around and thought, *Who's he talking about? I'm not a mighty hero. I'm hiding. I'm afraid.* The angel went on to tell him that he was to lead the charge and rescue the people of Israel from the Midianites, but Gideon started making a list of excuses, telling God what he wasn't. But I've learned that God won't ask you to do something if He hasn't already given you what you need. You may not have tapped into it yet, but it's in you.

As with Gideon, God is calling you a mighty hero. Other voices will call you ordinary, not talented, weak, afraid. Someone is wrong. These are two conflicting reports. You're either a mighty hero or you're weak and unable. Here's the key: You get to choose. Who do you say you are? Either voice can come to pass. It's all dependent on who you agree with. Are you going to agree with God and say, "Yes, I believe I'm a mighty hero. I'm equipped and empowered. I'm well able to fulfill my destiny"? Or are you going to do as Gideon did and start making excuses to stay where you are? "I wasn't raised in a good environment. I've had some bad breaks. This company did me wrong. This person walked out on me. Nobody would help me with my dream." Respectfully, none of that matters. What God has ordained for you cannot be stopped by people, by bad breaks, or by disappointments. God already knew it was going to happen. He's already lined up what you need. Now He's calling you a mighty hero. He's calling you to set new standards, to take your family to a new level. He's calling you a mighty hero to break generational curses that keep getting passed down, to put an end to that dysfunction. You are a mighty hero who will stop the poverty and lack and step into abundance and overflow.

> *You're either a mighty hero or you're weak and unable. Here's the key: You get to choose.*

What's interesting is that when God called Gideon a mighty hero, he hadn't done anything significant. He hadn't defeated a giant like David did, hadn't parted the Red Sea like Moses did, hadn't brought a dead person back to life like Elijah did. It seemed like he was just ordinary, just working on the farm every day, gathering up the wheat. But God calls us what we are before it happens. He knows what's in us. He's the One who put the potential, the gifts, and the talents inside. Gideon finally did what I'm asking us to do. Instead of seeing himself as ordinary, not able to lead an army, something rose up inside. He said in effect, "If God says I'm a mighty hero, then I believe I'm a mighty hero."

Gideon went out with 32,000 men to fight the Midianites, but God told him that was too many. He kept weeding it down more and more. Finally, when he just had three hundred men, he went out to fight this overwhelming army of thousands and thousands. Sometimes God will let the odds be against you in a great way, so when He turns it around, you'll know it's Him and not you. At midnight, Gideon and those three hundred men attacked the Midianites. They rushed to their camp shouting, "A sword for the Lord and a sword for Gideon." Here a few days earlier Gideon was hiding from his enemies, now he was rushing toward them with all the men shouting his name. God wanted Gideon to hear them declaring that he was a mighty hero. The Midianites got confused and started fighting one another. They ended up defeating themselves, and Gideon won the victory.

You Don't Need Everything You Think You Need

When God calls you a mighty hero, if you get in agreement with Him, you will become a mighty hero. He will make things happen that you couldn't make happen. Now quit discounting yourself. "If I had the training, if I came from a different family, if this pandemic hadn't hit, then I could do something great." God wants to do something great in your life despite the odds being against you. He's not limited by what you don't have, by what the economy is doing, or by what hasn't worked out. He doesn't need everything you think you need. He's going to cause you to accomplish great things with less resources. Just ask David—all he had was a slingshot and a few stones, but that catapulted him into his destiny.

God is calling you a giant killer, a history maker, a mighty hero. Why don't you get in agreement with Him? What a shame to live and die and never really know who you are. What could you become if you saw yourself the way God sees you? What dreams could you accomplish, what obstacles could you overcome, what businesses could you build, what books could you write, what influence could you have if you only knew who you are? Gideon didn't feel like a mighty hero. He didn't come from influence and wealth. He wasn't strong and courageous. Nothing about his circumstances looked like what God said. But God calls you what you are before you become it. Then it's up to you. If you believe it and get it down in your spirit, it will become a reality.

> *What a shame to live and die and never really know who you are.*

Gideon never dreamed that one day he would be in the Bible. He never dreamed thousands of years ago that we'd be talking about his story. You don't know where God is taking you. You don't know the doors He's going to open, the giants you're going to defeat, the influence you're going to have. There's an awesome future in front of you, but it's dependent on how you see yourself.

Who do you say you are? If you say average, limited, disadvantaged, or not able to, that will keep you from your destiny. Instead of letting people define you, instead of letting your past label you, why don't you go back to what God says about you? He's the One who made you. Like Gideon, you may not realize who you are. God sent an angel to remind him, then he rose up and left his mark. An angel may not appear to you, but maybe God is using me to remind you about who you are. You are a mighty hero, you are a masterpiece, you are strong, valuable, talented, confident, healthy, anointed, victorious, and forgiven. You are no ordinary child. Put your shoulders back, hold your head high, and step up to who you were created to be. If you do this, I believe and declare that you're going to see God show out in your life. New doors are about to open, with new opportunities. Giants are about to come down. You're about to see healing, favor, breakthroughs, and the fullness of your destiny.

CHAPTER SEVEN

Designed to Withstand

There are times in life when we can feel overwhelmed, like the pressure is too much. We go through a loss, we're dealing with a sickness, or we're not being treated right. A lady told me how things came against her at work. It looked as though she was going to lose her position. She said, "I can't take it anymore. The stress, the worry, the demands—it's too much to handle." She felt as though she was going to collapse under the weight of it, that it was unbearable. But the apostle Paul says, "God is faithful. He will not let you be tempted with more than you can bear. But with the temptation will make a way of escape so you can bear it." Paul was saying, "God will never let you face more pressure than you can handle. He won't let more weight come upon you than what you have the strength to bear."

When an architect designs a building, such as a big skyscraper, he doesn't just design what the outside is going to look like—the color, the style, the shape. That's important, but that will be of no use if he doesn't design the inner structure. He calculates all the loads, how much each floor will weigh, how much wind it will face, and how much equipment will be on it. Then he'll know how big the steel beams need to be, how deep the piers in the ground need to go, and how thick the foundation should be. In California, where there could be earthquakes, you have to put special reinforcements into the framing, more than in Texas. In Florida, the glass has to be able to withstand hurricane-force winds. The buildings there are different than the buildings in Iowa. When

> *The architect specifically designs each structure so it can withstand the pressure, so it can bear the weight, so it can endure outside elements.*

I was at a hotel in Colorado during the summer, I looked on the sloped roof and didn't know why it had so many wires and cables. I asked a hotel worker about it, and he said the cables were heated to melt the snow. He said that if they didn't keep the snow off, it could pile up and the weight would cause the roof to collapse. The architect specifically designs each structure so it can withstand the pressure, so it can bear the weight, so it can endure outside elements.

The good news is that your Architect is the Most High God. He not only designed planets, solar systems, and mountain ranges; He designed you. When He laid out the plan for your life, He calculated everything you would face—all the pressure, all the weight, all the winds. He took into account every hurt, every injustice, every loss, and every mistake that you would face. He designed your beams thick enough, your foundation deep enough, and He put in you the strength, the endurance, the fortitude, and the tenacity so that no matter what comes against you, it will not be too much to bear. You've been designed to withstand the winds, designed to outlast the opposition, designed to overcome the injustice, and designed to endure till the dream comes to pass.

God wouldn't be a just God if He knew you were going to face 120 mile per hour winds but only designed you for 80 mile per hour winds. That wouldn't even pass code. He couldn't get that design through the city planners. How much more has God designed you with exactly what you need? You may not be able to see it, but your beams are big enough, your walls are strong enough. You can bear whatever comes your way. God didn't miscalculate when He designed you. He didn't forget about the environment you would be in and the conditions you would face. He didn't make a mistake when He added up all the loads and pressures, and He didn't accidentally put in a beam that's too small. He designed you to handle that weight. Nothing you face will cause you to collapse under the weight of it. Thoughts may tell you, *It's too much. I can't handle this.* You need to remind yourself: "I've been designed to withstand. I have what it takes. I'm strong enough. I'm determined enough. I'm bold enough. I am well able."

Everything About You Was Carefully Planned

An architect doesn't wait until the pressure comes to see what kind of beams to put in. He doesn't wait until the middle of a storm, check the force of the winds, measure how much resistance is required, and then decide what kind of structure he needs to build. It's all calculated ahead of time. It's designed before one concrete truck shows up, before one hammer is lifted. The building specs have been studied, calculated, and approved before the construction ever starts. In the same way, before you were born, before you showed up on Planet Earth, your specs were carefully designed. Everything was strategically and precisely put in you for what you would need. When you face a big challenge, that means you have big beams, you have a strong infrastructure. You don't really know what's in you until you get some weight on you. You don't know what you can handle until pressure comes.

When something happens that we've never faced—a loss, a setback, a disappointment—it's tempting to think, *I can't handle this. It's overwhelming. It's going to sink me.* The truth is that you wouldn't be facing it unless you could handle it. If it was too much to bear, God wouldn't have allowed it. The very fact that it happened is a sign that you are well able. You may never have put that much pressure on the beams, and the

> *The reason you're tempted to feel overwhelmed is that you don't realize the structure was designed for that pressure.*

glass walls of your building may never have experienced winds so strong. The reason you're tempted to feel overwhelmed is that you don't realize the structure was designed for that pressure. But it's not a surprise to your Architect. He knew ahead of time, which is why He made the glass so strong. He took into account winds that you never knew you would encounter. Nothing you face can cause you to collapse. You've been designed to withstand.

Now, you can choose to collapse. In your mind, you can give up and think, *I'm overwhelmed, and life is too much.* That's why the Scripture tells us, "...so you don't faint in your mind." Your structure is strong enough, but you need to get your mind strong enough. Quit telling yourself, "It's too big. It's been this way too long, and I can't take it anymore." You are well able. No weapon formed against you will prosper. That difficulty didn't come to stay, it came to pass. Be strong and of good courage, for the Lord your God is with you.

To say we can't handle it is to say, "When God designed me, He miscalculated. He didn't make my foundation deep enough or He left out a beam. I can't carry this weight." God doesn't make mistakes. Psalm 139 says, "You have been fearfully and wonderfully made." That's not just talking about the outside—your looks, your personality, your talents. It's talking about your specs, your infrastructure, the way God designed things that you can't see. It's how He planned ahead of time for challenges and obstacles, things you think would overwhelm you, but out of nowhere strength rises up, a boldness comes on you, faith to overcome, a determination to stand strong and outlast the opposition.

You Have More Floors in You

When we acquired the Compaq Center, it didn't have any rooms for the children's and youth areas. It was a big sports arena, but we needed classrooms, a youth facility, and a chapel, so we built a five-story building on the end that connects with the lobbies. That's our family life center and offices. We told the architects that in the future we would want to add another five stories, because we're going to need more room. So they designed the foundation, the beams, the piers, and the underground structure so it can accommodate ten stories. It cost us more money, but we knew we had to build in the infrastructure if we were going to expand. If not, we would be limited.

When you look at our building, you see a five-story building. What you can't see unless you get the plans and look at the specs is that it's designed for ten stories. People driving down the freeway think the building is finished, that it's as tall as it ever will be. They don't know what's underground. What makes it capable of going higher is the weight the beams can hold, the thickness of the foundation. You may think you've reached your limits, and you've been at that level for a long time. Can I encourage you that you have more floors in you? Up until now, you've handled this much pressure fine, and you've gotten comfortable carrying this much weight—it's no problem. But if you could look at your specs, if you could see the plans God has for you, you would notice that your beams are much bigger than what you're carrying right now.

You could think that God overdesigned you, that He put something in that you don't need. No, it's coming. God has new levels. With that increase comes more weight. You're going to have more pressure, but not pressure in a bad sense. This is pressure that makes you stretch, makes you grow, makes you release your faith to believe bigger, dream bigger, and take on new challenges. It's not just difficulties; it's positive pressure that helps you discover that you can handle things you didn't think you could handle.

> *If you could see the plans God has for you, you would notice that your beams are much bigger than what you're carrying right now.*

Don't Lose the Battle in Your Mind

For seventeen years I worked behind the scenes at Lakewood doing the television production. In 1999, my father suddenly went to be with the Lord. I knew I was supposed to step up and pastor the church, but I didn't know how it was going to work out. I had never faced the pressure of having to get up to speak in front of thousands of people. Thoughts told me that I wasn't qualified and nobody was going to listen. On top of that, losing my father was traumatic. I had worked with him every day; we traveled the world together, and now he was gone. I should have been overwhelmed, the pressure should have caused me to shrink back and be discouraged. My whole world had turned upside down. But in the midst of all that turmoil, I felt a strength that I had never felt. It was a determination and a resilience that didn't make sense to my mind.

When I stepped up to minister, I was nervous and afraid, but deep down I believed I could do it. I knew I had what it takes. There was a boldness and confidence that I had never experienced. I realize now that wasn't just me being strong. I had been designed for this. I was designed to withstand the pressure and designed to overcome the loss. I discovered my beams were big enough, my foundation was strong enough. This didn't catch God off guard. What I'm saying is that you've been designed for everything you're going to face. When you face challenges that seem too big, too hard, too unfair, things that should cause you to collapse, don't worry. God knew they were coming. He's already taken that into account. He's already made your beams strong enough. You will be able to bear it. It may be uncomfortable, you may have to stretch, but the pressure is not going to stop you. You're going to discover ability that you didn't know you had.

Even now I have some opposition from critics, people who don't understand me, but it doesn't bother me anymore. I never pay attention to it. Life is good. For some people that criticism would cause them to be bitter, spiteful, and negative, but God gave me the grace to handle it. The pressure that would cause certain people to collapse doesn't affect me. Whatever is in your future, you have the grace to handle it. Nothing you face is beyond what you've been designed for. If you had told me when I was in my twenties and behind the scenes that one day I would be preaching every week and have to have something to say, or that we would have the Compaq Center and I would have been responsible to raise the funds and deal with the opposition, I would have thought, *There's no way. I can't carry that much weight. I would collapse.* It's because I couldn't see the infrastructure. I had never been put under that much pressure. But when it comes, as with me, you'll discover the beams are in place, your steel is thick enough, and your walls are strong enough. You can handle a lot more than you think you can handle.

> *Nothing you face is beyond what you've been designed for.*

The key is to not lose the battle in your mind. Your mind can keep you at five stories when you were designed for ten stories. Your mind can convince you the weight is too much. *Shrink back. It's not fair. You'll never overcome.* I might believe that if your architect lived down the street. You might convince me if he worked for a firm downtown. He may have made a mistake and miscalculated. But can I remind you that your Architect is the God who spoke worlds into existence, the God who designed planets, cosmos, and galaxies? He doesn't make mistakes. He doesn't miscalculate. You'll never face a situation for which you weren't designed. You'll never face pressure that will cause you to collapse, never face a problem that's too much, and never face a dream where you can't handle the weight.

There's a Skyscraper in You

When I look back over my life at all the critical points when I should have been overwhelmed, when I should have gotten stuck—my mother diagnosed with cancer, the death of my father, the lawsuit with the Compaq Center, having to raise a hundred million dollars to renovate the building—it was uncomfortable every time. I could have been stressed, weighted down, and given up, but I discovered that even though the pressure did not go away, I was designed to handle more pressure. I found out that I could bear more weight. If you don't face the pressure, you'll never discover who you really are. The higher you go, the more pressure there will be. The good news is that you have the beams to handle it. After a while, the pressure will subside and you'll find out that you are stronger than you think.

You can look back now at some of the things that overwhelmed you ten years ago and say as I do, "It's no big deal. I thought that trouble at work was going to give me a nervous breakdown, but I've come through it and now things like that don't bother me." It's not so much that God changed the circumstances; it's that God changed you. He showed you who you really are. You thought you'd always be five stories, but you better get ready, because there's a skyscraper in you. There are new levels, new giants to conquer, new mountains to climb, and new skills to learn. When the new comes—more pressure, more weight, more opposition—don't let it overwhelm you; let it inspire you. That means God's about to add a new floor. He's about to take you higher. You're going to discover ability that you didn't know you had.

> *When the new comes—more pressure, more weight, more opposition—don't let it overwhelm you; let it inspire you.*

"Joel, I didn't have a good childhood. I didn't have anyone encouraging me." That wasn't fair, but you have the beams to withstand it. You have the infrastructure to rise above it. That didn't stop your future. God didn't design your plan and overlook that you would have opposition early in life. He knew about it and took it into account. "I came down with this illness. I feel overwhelmed." The Scripture says, "Take hold of God's strength." It will be overwhelming if you don't remind yourself that this is not a surprise to God. He wouldn't have allowed it if you couldn't bear this weight. Since He did allow it, that means you're well able. Now all through the day take hold of that strength. "Father, thank You that I am strong in the Lord. Thank You that You're restoring health to me. Thank You that Your being for me is more than the world being against me."

The apostle Paul had all kinds of unfair things happen to him. Three times he was beaten with rods. He was put in prison without a trial. He was shipwrecked, spent the night on the open sea, and bitten by a poisonous snake. He could have collapsed under the pressure, been discouraged, lived overwhelmed. Yet he's the one who says, "Thanks be to God who always causes us to triumph." He understood that God doesn't let you face things that you can't handle. If you stay in faith you'll discover, as Paul did, that you've been designed to withstand the pressure. The enemy didn't come up with a scheme to outwit the God who created you. He can't send a storm that's so powerful that your walls get blown down. He can't put so much weight on you, so much pressure, that your beams can't hold up. Paul said, "We are hard pressed on every side, but not crushed." He was saying that we've been designed for the difficulty. Our Architect has taken into account all the weight, all the trouble, and all the bad breaks, and He's given you the strength, the courage, and the fortitude to withstand.

Your Beams Are Strong Enough

When he was a young man, David was anointed to be the next king of Israel. But afterward, he didn't go to the palace. He went back to the shepherds' fields and took care of his father's sheep for years. I'm sure thoughts told him, *You're never going to be the king. You're stuck out here. Nobody pays attention to you.* He could have been discouraged and lived sour, but he kept doing the right thing. He eventually defeated Goliath and went to the palace to serve King Saul. David was good to Saul, faithful and loyal, but Saul was jealous of David. He could see the favor on David's life. While David was playing the harp for Saul, trying to help him feel better, out of nowhere Saul threw a spear across the room, barely missing David. He had to take off running for his life. David spent years in the desert, hiding in caves, living on the run with Saul constantly on his trail. David thought it had been difficult and lonely in the shepherds' fields, all those years feeling left out, but he had never experienced this kind of pressure—the king trying to kill him. He'd done nothing wrong. He could have been overwhelmed, let the pressure break him, cause him to give up and ride off into the sunset, but David's attitude was: *I've been designed to withstand this injustice. God wouldn't have allowed it if I wasn't designed to handle this pressure.*

On the way to your destiny, there will be opposition, things that are not fair, people who should be for you but turn against you. You have to remind yourself that you can handle it. You've been designed for it. You're not going to collapse under that weight. Your beams are strong enough. You don't have to get revenge, and you don't have to live bitter. You can forgive, you can take the high road, and you can overlook an insult. It may not be fair, but you've been designed to withstand the injustice as David was, and you've been designed to outlast the opposition. If David had complained about being stuck in the shepherds' fields or been overwhelmed by King Saul and let the pressure sour his life, we wouldn't be talking about him. He understood that nothing he faced would be too much to bear. He didn't like it, it wasn't comfortable, but he didn't let the pressure discourage him and cause him to miss his destiny.

We all face pressure. We all have times when we can feel overwhelmed and think it's too much. The reason you have big opposition is because you have a big destiny. The good news is that God took that all into account when He designed your infrastructure. He didn't

> *The reason you have big opposition is because you have a big destiny.*

give you a big future with weak walls, with a small foundation, with little beams. You have what it takes. You are stronger than you think. You have more endurance, more stamina, more grace, more forgiveness. Those challenges are a sign that there are more floors in you. You have a big foundation. God is getting you ready to go higher, to see new levels of influence and favor. Don't complain about the difficult times—that's when you discover what's in you. David discovered perseverance, courage, and faith as he had never seen. If you keep the right attitude, instead of breaking you, the pressure will develop you. You'll grow and mature so you can take your throne.

Maybe you're in a test now. You think it's too much to bear. "These people at work are not fair. This situation with my child has me overwhelmed. This illness I'm dealing with is stressing me out." Have a new perspective. You've been designed to withstand. You already have what you need. Take hold of His strength. Instead of thinking about how difficult it is, turn it around and say, "I can do all things through Christ. I've been armed with strength for this battle. I'm anointed for difficult times. I may walk through the valley of the shadow of death, but I know a secret: I'm not staying here. This valley is not my home. I'm coming out better, stronger, victorious, into new levels of my destiny."

You Have the Infrastructure to Take You Higher

A friend of mine came to see our church building. He's an engineer. I took him through the lobbies and auditorium. I brought him up on the platform, showed him the lights, the sound system, the big screens, and how the band pit goes up and down. All those are things that impress me, and he liked it, but he asked something that no one else has ever asked me. He said, "Can I see the mechanical rooms?" I asked, "The what?" He said, "The mechanical areas, the power plant, the heating and cooling systems, the chilled water pipes." I didn't even know where those were. I had to get my brother-in-law Kevin to take us to these areas of the building that I had never seen. He brought us through huge rooms full of equipment, with generators, pumps, and electrical panels. He showed us the steel beams that allow the building to span over a hundred yards without a column. My engineer friend couldn't believe it. He stood there in awe, marveling over the turbines on a huge pump and talking with Kevin about things I knew nothing about. I left that day with a new appreciation for the building. It has all kinds of things behind the scenes, infrastructure we can't see, design that makes what we can see so amazing.

In the same way, God has put incredible things in you that you can't see. You don't realize all that you're capable of. You have beams that allow you to go further than where you are now. You have infrastructure to take you to higher levels, to add new floors. God didn't design you to reach a certain level and stay there. You may be at five stories now, you're doing well,

> *What you can't see is you have a ten-story foundation.*

and God's blessed you. What you can't see is you have a ten-story foundation. Where you are is not your final destination. God says, "The path of the righteous gets brighter and brighter." He not only designed you to increase but to withstand the winds, to outlast the opposition, to overcome unfair situations. As you take new ground, there will be new obstacles. The greater the opportunity, the greater the opposition. In religious terms, new levels, new devils.

Whatever you face, remind yourself that you can handle it. Not because you're so great, but because your Architect, the Most High God, designed you with everything you need. He promised you'll never face anything that you can't bear. When you're tempted to think, *Life is overwhelming. This is too much. I can't handle it,* you need to see your mechanical rooms. If you could only see what God put in you—the courage, the strength, the determination, the fortitude—you would realize you can handle it, you've been designed to withstand. I believe and declare strength is coming into you, courage is rising up. God is breathing new life into your spirit. You will withstand every storm, outlast every attack, overcome every obstacle, and become everything God created you to be.

CHAPTER EIGHT

Overcoming Weariness

As we're going through life, fighting the good fight of faith, one challenge we all have to face is weariness. It's easy to get tired. To be weary means to lose your sense of pleasure, to not feel the enjoyment that you should. You can be raising great children, but because you're weary, you're not enjoying them. You can have the job of your dreams, you worked hard to get there, but weariness has set in and you're not passionate about it anymore. Sometimes we become weary because the battle is taking longer than we thought. A lady who was in town recently for her checkup at the cancer hospital came to one of our services. She had hoped this would be her last treatment, but she found out she had to take it for another six months. She was very disappointed and said, "I don't think I can go through this again."

When the battle is taking longer than expected, when we're working hard but not seeing increase, when we're believing for a baby but year after year goes by and we're still not pregnant, weariness will come. If the enemy can't take you out all at once, his next strategy is to try to wear you down. Many people are suffering from battle fatigue. They've been standing a long time, trying to break the addiction, believing for the promotion, but it hasn't happened yet. They didn't think they'd still be single, still dealing with the sickness, or still trying to get the loan. Now they're tired.

The apostle Paul says in Galatians 6, "Don't get weary in well-doing." God knew weariness would come, otherwise He wouldn't have told us to not get weary. He says to not get weary in well-doing. That means you're doing the right thing but not getting the right results. It doesn't seem as though it's making

> *Weariness cannot automatically come; you have to open the door.*

a difference. Let me encourage you that your time is coming. Your due season is on the way. Don't let time talk you out of it, don't let discouragement cause you to give up, don't let negative thoughts convince you to settle where you are. Your mind will give you good excuses. Thoughts will tell you, *I'm too tired to fight this addiction. I'm too tired to believe for my marriage. I'm too tired to stretch to the next level. I've been doing it for so long.* If you dwell on those thoughts, you'll allow weariness in. You'll become more tired, more discouraged, and more negative. Weariness cannot automatically come; you have to open the door. When thoughts tell you, *It's never going to change. It's been too long,* instead of dwelling on that, just say, "No, thanks. I know that God is still on the throne. I know my time is coming. I've been armed with strength for this battle. I can do all things through Christ. I am strong in the Lord." The psalmist says to "take hold of God's strength." It's available, but you have to take hold of it.

Don't Allow Weariness In

This is what David did. He was doing the right thing, but the wrong thing kept happening. Even after Samuel had anointed him to be the next king, his family looked down on him and treated him like he was second-class. He could have been sour and upset, but instead he kept taking care of his father's sheep, doing it with excellence. How did David keep going strong? I can hear him under his breath reminding himself, "Don't get weary in well-doing." When he was being good to King Saul, playing the harp to try to make him feel better, Saul threw a spear at him and tried to kill him. David could have been frustrated and thought, *What's the use? I'm being my best, and this man tries to take my life.* Instead he kept telling himself, "Don't get weary in well-doing." Saul ended up chasing him through the desert for years. David had to live on the run, hiding in caves as a fugitive. He could have said, "God, this is not fair. Where is Your justice? I thought I was supposed to be the king." Again and again he kept that phrase playing in his mind, "Don't get weary in well-doing."

David understood this principle: When you give in to weariness, you lose your strength. When you start thinking, *I'm too tired. It's never going to work out. This is not fair,* the energy you need to keep moving forward is drained out. I'm not saying that we will never feel weariness; it will come to us. I'm saying don't allow it in. When you believe those lies that say, "This is too much

> *When it's the most difficult, when you face the greatest temptation to settle, that means the victory is near.*

for me. I've been doing this so long. What's the use? It's never going to change," that will keep you from your destiny. When you're weary, you don't have the passion, the strength, and the determination to fight the good fight. Don't let battle fatigue keep you from your victory. Don't let weariness stop your dream from coming to pass. You are closer than you think. When it's the most difficult, when you face the greatest temptation to settle, that means the victory is near. The breakthrough, the healing, or the promotion is about to show up. Your due season is close.

David had been anointed by Samuel as a teenager to be the next king of Israel. Thirteen years went by, and there was no sign of it happening. One day when he and his six hundred men came home from a time of service to the king of Gath, they found their city had been attacked and burned. All their possessions had been carried away, and their families had been taken captive. It was the worst defeat of David's life. His darkest hour. The Scripture says he and his men wept until they could not weep anymore. David was depressed and discouraged, and his own men talked of stoning him. I'm sure he was tempted to think, *God, this is the final straw. I'm tired. I've been doing the right thing year after year. I can't take it anymore. I'm done.* Weariness comes to us all. David could have given up, and that would be the end of his story. He would never have taken the throne and never seen the promise come to pass. But when he was tired, when he felt like throwing in the towel, he did what we all must do. He dug his heels in and said, "I've come too far to stop now."

The Scripture says in 1 Samuel 30, "David encouraged himself in the Lord his God." He made a decision and said, "I am not allowing this weariness to stay. I'm going to stir up my faith." While the other men were weeping, discouraged, and complaining, I can hear David saying, "I am strong in the Lord. I am anointed. I am well able. The forces for me are greater than the forces against me." You can talk yourself into defeat or you can talk yourself into victory. When you speak to yourself the right way, strength comes, courage comes, vision comes, healing comes. Every time you say, "This is too hard," you're getting weaker. When you whisper, "I can't take this anymore," strength is leaving. When you say, "I'm so disappointed. I can't believe this happened," you're inviting discouragement.

But when you say, "I am well able," you're inviting strength. When you declare, "I can do all things through Christ," you're inviting favor. You may feel tired, but don't verbalize it. Don't give it life by speaking it out. The Scripture says, "Let the weak say, 'I am strong.'" It doesn't say let the weak talk about their weakness, or let the sick talk about the sickness, or let the disappointed talk about the bad break. Turn it around and say, "Yes, this is tough, but I am strong in the Lord. God is breathing in my direction. No weapon formed against me will prosper." That's what it means to take hold of His strength.

Take Hold of His Strength

Today you may be dealing with battle fatigue. It's taking longer than you thought. You're tired of fighting, and you don't think you can go on. God wants to breathe new life into your dreams. He says, "Come to Me when you're weary, and I will give you rest." You don't have to do it on your own. You can take hold of His strength. It starts in your mind. The prophet Isaiah says, "If you wait upon the Lord, He will renew your strength. You will mount up with wings like an eagle's. You will run and not be weary, you will walk and not faint." To wait upon the Lord doesn't mean to sit back passively, to be idle and say, "Okay, God, do it. I'm tired. I'm worn-out. Renew my strength." Those who *wait* are described in one version as "those who look for God's goodness, who expect His favor, who long for His blessing." Waiting is supposed to be active. "Lord, I thank You that You're turning this situation around. Thank You that You're bigger than this cancer, stronger than these people who are coming against me. Thank You that You're bringing my dreams to pass."

You won't soar like an eagle if you're negative in your thinking. You won't run and not be weary if you're focused on your problems and thinking about how impossible it is. What causes your strength

> *You won't soar like an eagle if you're negative in your thinking.*

to be renewed is when you live with expectancy, when you have this hope that God is working in your life. It's when you have this knowing that He's in control, that He will get you to where you're supposed to be. When you come to Him, you get your thoughts going in the right direction, and He'll give you rest. You don't have to live weary. You can get your passion back. Nothing that's happened to you has stopped God's plan. As with David, it may be taking a long time, and you may have had some bad breaks, but God is still on the throne. He knows how to get you to your destiny.

David not only stirred himself up, but he got his men stirred back up. They went out and attacked the enemy and recovered everything that was stolen. Three days later, King Saul was killed in battle by the Philistines, and David was anointed to be the king of Judah. That was thirteen years after Samuel had anointed David as king. Here's my point: He was closest to his victory when he faced his greatest challenge. Stay encouraged when it seems as though everything is coming against you, when it's taken a long time and now you're facing a new problem—the medical report is not good, business went down, or the situation at work intensified. When weariness is trying to overtake you, that's a sign that you're close to your victory and things are about to turn around. The breakthrough is on the way, the promotion is coming, the healing is coming. Don't get weary in well-doing. It may not happen overnight. You have to do as David did and be in it for the long haul. During those thirteen years when he waited for the promise, he had to deal with battle fatigue. Thoughts told him, *It's never going to happen. You wouldn't have these challenges if you were going to be the king. Samuel must have gotten it wrong.* Weariness came knocking on his door again and again. The reason David saw the promise fulfilled is not because he never felt weariness, not because he was superhuman and was never tempted to get tired. It was because he didn't allow that weariness in.

When you've been in a battle for a long time, you have to be especially on guard. It's easy to get discouraged and think, *I'm tired of standing strong. I'm tired of fighting this illness. I'm tired of believing for my dreams.* When you feel that weariness, instead of giving in you have to learn to look up and say, "God, I'm asking You to renew my strength." The moment you ask, you'll feel

> The moment you ask, you'll feel strength come into you.

strength come into you. God will breathe new life into your spirit. He'll cause you to mount up with wings like an eagle's. You may be tired today after having dealt with a challenge in your health, your finances, or a relationship for many years. You used to believe you would overcome it, but it's been so long, and you feel worn-out. You don't think it's ever going to happen. Let me encourage you that what God promised, He's still going to bring to pass. You may have given up, but He hasn't given up. He still has your healing, your promotion, the right person. Do your part and get your fire back. Start taking hold of His strength. Don't allow that weariness in. The enemy wouldn't be fighting you so hard unless he knew you were close to your victory. He couldn't take you out, so he's trying to wear you out, to get you discouraged and weary. Don't fall into that trap. All through the day, you have to say, "Lord, I thank You that You're renewing my strength. Thank You that I am strong in the Lord. Thank You that I will soar like an eagle." That battle may be taking a long time, but right now I believe that strength is coming into you, hope is coming into you. God is filling you with fresh vision, with fresh courage, with energy, with vitality. You will run and not be weary. You will walk and not faint.

Mount Up with Wings Like Eagles

A friend of mine was diagnosed with cancer of the brain. The doctors gave him only six months to live. It was the worst kind of brain cancer you can have. He had surgery to remove the tumor, which was successful, but another one developed. He's been taking all the treatments. He changed his diet and has been very disciplined about what he eats. He made it past the first six months, then another, and another. Every time I see him, he's upbeat, has a smile, and still has his sense of humor. He's full of faith and resolve. He's coming up on three years since his diagnosis. The other day, they took a new brain scan and couldn't find any sign of a tumor. My friend has a very prestigious doctor, one of the world leaders in that field. He asked my friend if he would go to a support group for people who have brain cancer. My friend said, "Doctor, I don't feel like I need to go. I'm fine." The doctor said, "I'm not asking you to go for your sake. I'm asking you to go for other people's sake, so they will see someone who has beaten the odds." His doctor wanted him to go as an example, to be a source of encouragement for others. God wants to do that for you. He wants to make you an example of His goodness.

But throughout my friend's last three years, there were plenty of times he was tempted to get weary. The initial news, of course, was devastating. He never thought he would be dealing with brain cancer. It went away once and then came back, which was followed by another surgery. He could have thought, *I can't deal with this anymore. It's not meant to be.* But he didn't allow the

> *Don't let weariness talk you out of standing strong. Don't let battle fatigue convince you to give up.*

weariness in. He kept believing, kept praying, and kept doing what he could. Because he didn't get weary in well-doing, God caused him to mount up with wings like an eagle's. He became an exception. That's what happens when you don't give in to battle fatigue. You may be facing a situation like his that looks impossible, and you could easily let it overwhelm you. God has given you strength for that battle. He said you would never face something that you couldn't handle. Quit telling yourself that it's too much, and start taking hold of His strength. That cancer, that legal problem, or that situation in your finances is no match for you. It may look permanent, but it's just a matter of time before God turns it around. Don't let weariness talk you out of standing strong. Don't let battle fatigue convince you to give up. It may be taking a long time, but as with David, the promise is on the way. If you stay in faith, God will not only renew your strength, He'll renew your health, renew your marriage, restore your business. He'll make a way where you don't see a way.

Live Balanced

In 1 Kings 18, the prophet Elijah asked King Ahab to bring out the four hundred and fifty false prophets that worshipped the god Baal. Elijah said to them, "Let's have a contest to see whose God is real." They both cut up sacrificial pieces of meat and placed them on the wood of separate altars. The God who started the wood on fire would be the true God. Elijah let the prophets of Baal go first. They prayed, danced, chanted hour after hour, louder and louder, but nothing happened. When it was Elijah's turn, he called them all to come near him and asked them to gather around. When he prayed, fire came down from Heaven like a great bolt of lightning and burned up the sacrifice, the wood, and even the stone altar. Those false prophets fell facedown, frightened to death. In response, the people of Israel who saw it killed all the false prophets. It was a great victory for Elijah.

But when King Ahab's wife, Jezebel, heard what had happened to her false prophets, she was furious. As we read in Chapter 1, she sent word to Elijah, saying, "May the gods strike me and even kill me if I haven't killed you by this time tomorrow." He ended up running way into the desert to escape, finally so exhausted that he sat down under a tree. He was so depressed that he prayed that he would die. Elijah said, "God, I've had enough. I'm done. Take my life."

Here is this incredible man of faith, one of the great heroes in the Bible. He had seen God raise a child from the dead, he'd prayed and it rained after a three-and-a-half year drought, he called down fire from Heaven, he had outrun Ahab's chariot. But now because of one angry woman, he wanted to end his life. He was depressed, discouraged, not wanting to go on, and he fell asleep. While he was sleeping, an angel appeared and woke him up. Usually when an angel showed up, it was to open prison doors, or to part a Red Sea, or close the mouths of lions. But this angel woke him up and did something interesting. He said, "Elijah, get up and eat." Elijah looked up and saw bread baking over hot coals, and a jar of water. He ate the bread and drank the water, then went back to sleep. A little later, the angel came back, woke him up again, and said the same thing, "Get up and eat." Elijah ate and drank some more. The Scripture says that strengthened by that food, he traveled forty days to his next assignment. His whole attitude had changed.

Why was Elijah depressed, discouraged, and not wanting to go on? He was tired, he was hungry, he was worn-out, and he needed some sleep. Sometimes when we're weary, it's not about a spiritual problem, it's a physical problem. Elijah had just run for twenty-four hours, trying to get away from Jezebel. He didn't need a miracle; he just needed some rest. He just needed a good meal. The angel

didn't touch him and say, "Elijah, be healed from your weariness,
be free from the depression." No, he

> *Sometimes when we're weary, it's not about a spiritual problem, it's a physical problem.*

said, "Eat this food, and drink this water." He was saying, "Take care of yourself. Get back in balance." Too often we're fighting battles in our mind, we're discouraged and have no passion, not because of the enemy, but because of how poorly we're taking care of ourselves.

You're a three-part being—spiritual, physical, and emotional. You have to take care of each one. You can pray for twenty-four hours a day, but you're not going to feel well physically. Your body needs to be cared for. You can go to the gym and work out five hours a day, seven days a week, but if you're not taking time for your spiritual and emotional side, you're not going to be your best. You need to take care of all three parts. Living balanced is the key. You can't stay up all night and not get proper sleep and expect to feel well. You're not going to have the passion you need. You won't make good decisions. Some people are discouraged, don't have any energy, and they're praying for a miracle. If the angel showed up, he would say what he did to Elijah, "Get some sleep. Start eating better. Take care of your physical body." You can't drink twenty cups of coffee a day, eat sugar and junk food all the time, and expect to feel well.

Take Care of Your Temple

I read that one of the main causes of depression is not getting enough sleep. What am I saying? Pay attention to the practical things. You can't go against natural laws and expect God to bless you. Your body is the house you live in. The Scripture says your body is the temple of the Holy Spirit. Take care of your temple. Don't put junk in your temple. Your spirit cannot live on this Earth without your body. We need you here a long time. Don't have your life cut short because you didn't take care of what God has given you. It's easy to work all the time. It's easy to get up early and stay up late, to always be thinking about business and what you need to fix, something else to take care of. That's doing yourself and the people around you a disservice. Your mind needs a break, and your body needs to relax. That's why God required the people in the Old Testament to take a Sabbath. One day a week they were not to even pick up a stick. They had to rest. Even when God created the universe, on the seventh day He rested. He didn't have to rest, because He's God, but He was showing us this principle.

David said in Psalm 23, "He makes me to lie down in green pastures, He leads me beside the still waters." It's interesting that he says, "He makes me lie down." That means that if you don't take care of yourself—if you live stressed-out, overworked, run-down, and you don't eat right, don't sleep enough—eventually God will make you lie down in the green pastures. You'll probably

> *Don't wear yourself out to where God has to make you slow down.*

come to a point where you have to rest. Don't wear yourself out to where God has to make you slow down. Too many times we end up unhealthy and not able to do what we used to. It wasn't the enemy; it was the fact that we didn't take care of our temple.

You need recreation. You need to laugh and have fun. Laughter is medicine. Laughter releases stress and causes you to have more energy. My personality type is that I'm a hard worker, I'm driven, I'm determined, I like to accomplish things. We have so much going on that I could think about the ministry and what to do next for twenty-four hours a day. But I've learned that if I don't take time to exercise each week, I'm not going to be my best when I preach on the weekends. If I don't take time to have fun with my family, go on bike rides, and play basketball, I'm not going to function at my highest level. You will be your most productive, your most effective, not when you're working all the time, not when you're putting in the most hours, but when you're balanced physically, spiritually, and emotionally. If you neglect one area, it will lessen what you can accomplish.

Many people are good at taking care of the physical and the emotional, but they don't take care of the spiritual. There's no connection to God. Your life will be more

> *If you want to reach your highest potential, take care of the total you.*

rewarding and more fulfilling when you're in relationship with your Creator. He breathed life into you. He knows your purpose. He knows what you can accomplish. When you make Him a part of your life, you'll go further than you can in just your own ability and talent. The Scripture says, "If you put Him first place, He'll crown your efforts with success." His favor on your life will take you where your talent could not take you. If you want to reach your highest potential, take care of the total you. Make your spiritual life a priority. When you get up in the morning, take time to thank God for the day. Don't run out of the house stressed out, in a hurry. Start the day off with a grateful attitude. Read the Scripture, meditate on His promises, and fill your mind with thoughts of faith, hope, and victory.

You don't have to go through life weary. Maybe you need to make a practical adjustment today like Elijah did and start taking care of yourself. Or maybe it's a change in your attitude, in how you're seeing things. Weariness comes to us all, but you don't have to allow it in. You may have been in a challenge a long time. You're struggling with battle fatigue. This is a new day. God is breathing new life into your dreams. Dare to take hold of His strength. Get your fire back. When you feel weak, start declaring, "I am strong." If you do this, I believe and declare you're going to run and not be weary. Courage is coming, energy is coming, vitality is coming. God is renewing your strength so you can soar like the eagles.

CHAPTER NINE

You're Still Going to Get There

We all have dreams and goals, things we know God has promised us. We start off excited. We're sailing along fine, making progress, then a storm arises—an unexpected challenge, a sickness, a breakup, we lose a loved one, or a contract we were counting on doesn't go through. It's easy to get discouraged and think that it's never going to happen. But God doesn't promise something and then change His mind. He doesn't put a dream in your heart and then take it back. What He starts, He finishes. You may not see a way, but God hasn't run out of options. We think in the natural, but God is supernatural. He has ways we've never thought of. He wouldn't have allowed that storm if it was going to keep you from your destiny. If that bad break, that person who walked away, or that loss was going to stop your purpose, God would have kept it from happening. You may not like it, but it's a part of the process. Storms come to us all. The good news is, God is in control of the winds. He's in control of what's trying to stop you. All He has to do is shift the winds and instead of holding you back, they will thrust you forward. They were meant to harm you, but God knows how to turn it around and use it to advance you.

You may be in a situation in your health, your marriage, or your finances where you don't see how it could work out. Every voice says, "There's no way. It's too late. The obstacles are too big." God is saying, "You're still going to there. I'm still on the throne, and I'm working behind the scenes. I'm fighting your battles. I'm lining up the breaks you need. I'm arranging the right people." When it's all said and

> *Will you trust Him even though the winds are howling and you don't see any sign of it improving?*

done, what God promised will come to pass. You're still going to get well, you're still going to meet the right person, you're still going to see your family restored, you're still going to accomplish your dream. Where you are is not an accident. God is directing your steps. He may not have sent the storm, but He is in control of the storm. Here's the test: Will you trust Him even though the winds are howling and you don't see any sign of it improving? Will you stay in faith even though every thought says it's never going to work out?

Mix Faith with the Promises

This is what the apostle Paul did in Acts 27. He was a prisoner on a boat that was headed to Rome. He had been arrested in Jerusalem, having been falsely accused of causing a disturbance. Even though he was found not guilty, he appealed his case to Caesar. As they were sailing on this several-month journey, a huge storm arose with hurricane-force winds. The waves were huge, tossing the boat up and down. For fourteen days it didn't let up. They didn't see the sun or the stars. The boat had gotten so torn up that it was taking on water. The crew started throwing the cargo and supplies overboard. They had even quit eating. The Scripture says, "All hope was gone." They were convinced they were going to die. But in the midst of this storm, an angel appeared to Paul and said, "Don't be afraid, Paul, for you will surely stand before Caesar. What's more, God in His goodness has granted safety to everyone sailing with you."

Paul had this promise that he would make it to Rome, but all the circumstances said it would never happen. Everywhere he looked— the winds, the waves, the crew—said he was not going to make it. He could have thought, *God, I must have heard You wrong. I thought You said I'd stand before Caesar, but I'm on a sinking boat, out in the middle of the sea, stuck in a hurricane.* Sometimes what God promised looks just the opposite of what we see. "God, You said I was going to get well, but all I see is sickness. You said I would lend and not borrow, but I see lack, struggle, and debt. You said my children would be mighty in the land, but I see compromise and addictions." You can't be moved by what you see; you have to be moved by what you know. Don't let circumstances talk you out of what God spoke to you.

When it looked impossible, with no sign of things improving, Paul went before the crew and said, "It's going to be all right, so get something to eat. God promised that not only would I stand before Caesar, but that everyone sailing with me would be saved." The next verse is the

> "I believe it will be just as God said."

key. He said, "I believe it will be just as God said." God can make all kinds of promises, but unless you take this next step and say as Paul did, "I believe what God said will come to pass," those promises won't do you any good. You have to mix faith with it. When Paul told the crew they were all going to be saved, there's no doubt that waves were splashing him in the face, the wind was almost knocking him down, and he had to hold on to something firm in order to stand up. It had been like that for two weeks. Paul could have been depressed and complaining like the rest of them, but he was talking about what God promised. He was speaking life in the face of death, he was talking victory in the middle of defeat. What you're saying in the storm is going to have a great impact on whether or not you get out of it.

If you're saying, "I'll never get well. Did you see the report? I'll never break this addiction. I've had it since high school. The people who did me wrong, the betrayal, and the injustice have ruined my life." If you talk defeat, you're going to have defeat. If you think you'll never get out of a trouble, you'll never get out. In the middle of the storm, you need to declare what God promised. "I'm coming out. This too shall pass. I don't see a way, but I'm not moved by what I see. I'm not worried about the winds or the waves, the people who are trying to stop me. I believe what God said will come to pass. I will get well, I will prosper and succeed, and my children will serve the Lord." Get in agreement with God.

You're a Paul

The angel said, "Paul, everyone sailing with you will be saved." It's interesting that Paul was the prisoner. He had no authority or influence on that boat. The others saw him as insignificant, as secondary, "just another convict we have to transport." They thought Paul was sailing with them, but God said, "Paul, everyone sailing with you will be saved." The enemies who look down on you think they have the upper hand. Don't worry, because you're not sailing with them, they're sailing with you. God has you

> *You may be on their boat, but remember that they're sailing with you.*

in the palms of His hands. Nothing can snatch you away. You may be in the boat of the opposition, so to speak. It seems as though you're at a disadvantage at work or at school, but people don't determine your destiny. They can't stop God's plan for your life. You may be on their boat, but remember that they're sailing with you. God is going to get you to where you're supposed to be.

Without Paul on that boat, all the people would have perished. The hurricane would have caused it to sink. There was no chance in the natural. All the circumstances said it was doomed. It would have looked like just bad luck. But there was a man on the boat with a calling on his life, a man with a purpose, with a destiny. God is showing us that a storm cannot stop what God has purposed. You may be in a situation that doesn't look good, it would stop most people, but it can't stop you. Why? You're a Paul. You have a purpose, you have an assignment. There is a calling on your life, something God has ordained for you to accomplish. You're not just filling up space, you're a person of destiny. There's a Caesar whom you've been called to stand before. There's a dream God put in your heart—that's not an option, for God has purposed it. He's already lined up what you need. There's a giant you've been called to defeat—a generational curse, something that's held your family back.

That's why the storm is so bad. The enemy wants you to give up, get discouraged, and think, *I didn't hear God right*. No, that storm is not keeping you from your destiny; it's a sign you're close to your destiny. The enemy wouldn't be sending the winds, the rain, the opposition, the trouble, or the sickness if he didn't know Caesar was right up ahead. What you've been called to do—your greatest victory, your greatest accomplishment, something more than you've imagined, new levels of influence, favor, abundance, and freedom that your family has never seen—is right past this storm. The reason it can't defeat you is because you're a Paul. The destiny in you is bigger than the storm around you. The purpose in you cannot be stopped by the waves, by people, by opposition. Stay in faith. Keep declaring what God said about you. "I will stand before Caesar. I will fulfill my destiny. I will set new standards for my family. I will pay my house off. I will keep my marriage together. I will break this cycle of defeat, dysfunction, depression, and poverty that has been passed down. I will take new ground."

Don't Let the Storm Talk You Out of It

If you're going to come out of the storm, you have to know you're a Paul. You're not just drifting around; there's a calling on your life. The enemy knows it. He wouldn't be fighting you if he didn't know you were destined to do great things. He knows it, and God knows it; now make sure you know it. What God has spoken over your life wasn't just a nice thought, it wasn't just something that He hopes will happen; it's a command. "Paul, you will stand before Caesar." He didn't say, "I think you will, if the weather holds up, if these people don't get upset, if you have the funds." When God speaks, it's not the storm, not the opposition, not your boss, not the addiction, not the lack of funds, and not the enemy that can keep it from happening. The only thing that can is if we don't believe.

> *What God has spoken over your life wasn't just a nice thought, it wasn't just something that He hopes will happen; it's a command.*

God works where there's faith. If Paul had said, "God, I don't see how I can stand before Caesar. I'm a prisoner. These people don't like me, and I'm in a hurricane," he would have let the doubt stop his purpose. Don't let that storm talk you out of your destiny. You don't have to see how it's going to happen. All you have to do is believe. In the face of the opposition, with the winds and the rain coming against you, dare to say as Paul did, "God, I believe just what You promised will come to pass."

Look how good God is. He told Paul that all those who were sailing with him had been granted safety. Even Paul's enemies, the Roman soldiers who wanted to kill the prisoners to prevent them from escaping, had the promise that their life would be spared. Now if it was up to us, we'd say, "God, wipe them out. Pay them back. Let them suffer." But God is not like us. He's so merciful that some of your enemies will be blessed because of you. When the favor on your life helps them go further, they'll have a change of heart. They won't be against you, they'll be for you. Instead of pushing you down, they'll push you up.

After two weeks of being battered by this storm, one morning they noticed an island with a bay off in the distance. They tried to steer that way but the winds were too strong. When they got close, the boat hit a sandbar and broke apart. Now they were all in the water. They grabbed pieces of the boat and began to swim for the shore. In a few hours, all 276 people had made it safely to the island. Not one person lost their life. When they hit the bottom and the boat broke apart, I'm sure some of them panicked and thought, *That's it. We're done. The boat is gone. Now we don't have a chance.* But they made it to the shore without the boat. God is saying, "You're going to make it without what you thought you had to have. You're going to make it without what you lost, you're going to make it without what didn't work out."

You Don't Have to Have the Boat

I was very close with my father. I worked with him for seventeen years, and we traveled the world together. I used to think, *What am I going to do when my father is gone?* In 1999, he suddenly died. I still miss my father, but now I realize that I made it without my father, I made it without going to seminary, I made it without the formal training. I thought I had to have all of these things, but I didn't need them. When I stepped up to pastor the church, most of the people were for me, but there were a few people whom I had known for years who had been very supportive of my father but weren't supportive of me. They loved me, but they just wanted me to do things their way. I've learned you have to be you. There's no anointing on your life to be like someone else. You are anointed to be you. At first it bothered me that they weren't for me, and I was tempted to worry about what would happen if they left the church, if they didn't support me. Eventually they did leave. But things didn't fall apart. I made it without their support. I made it without their encouragement. I made it without the boat.

Sometimes God will take things away that we think we need so that we have to depend on Him and not people, not the contract, not the job. Can I tell you that you're going to make it without that person who walked away, without that friend who betrayed you, without that spouse who left? I know it's painful, but they weren't your savior; you already have a Savior. He has you in

> *As long as you're looking back, focused on what you lost... then you're going to miss the new things God has in store.*

the palms of His hands. If they left you, you didn't need them. If you had to have them to fulfill your purpose, they would have stayed. You have to accept that they're not a part of your destiny and move forward. As long as you're looking back, focused on what you lost, who didn't stay, why the boat fell apart, then you're going to miss the new things God has in store. You can still make it to the shore. It just may not be the way you were thinking. God's ways are not our ways. We can get so set on how we think it's going to happen, and what we think we need, and who's going to be there, that we get discouraged if it doesn't fit into our plan. Stay open. God knows what He's doing.

You're going to make it without that contract that didn't go through. You worked hard, but they didn't choose you. You deserved the promotion, but you were passed over. That's not the end. God has something better. The boat may have broken apart, but you don't have to have the boat. God knows how to open new doors, to cause contracts and promotions to find you. Don't settle there and think, *Just my luck. I never get any good breaks. Why did this happen to me?* It happened because there's a calling on your life. There are new levels in your future. The good news is that storm can't stop you. God knows how to get you to the shore, but it may be through an unconventional way, a way that is out of the ordinary. It may happen without the boat, and you may have to swim to shore, but the grace will be there to do it.

You're going to make it without that loved one you lost. Sure you miss them, but that didn't cancel your destiny. It may seem like the end, but really it's a new beginning. You are stronger than you think, you have more in you than you think—more talent, more determination, more courage. God is not going to leave you in that storm. The boat may have broken apart, but you're closer to the shore than you think.

> *The boat may have broken apart, but you're closer to the shore than you think.*

Grab On to the Broken Pieces

David made it to the king's throne without his family believing in him. I'm sure he was discouraged when his father didn't call him in from the shepherds' fields when Samuel came to choose one of the sons to be the next king. He was tempted to be offended when his older brother made fun of him for being the smallest and having to take care of their father's sheep. He could have thought, *God, this isn't fair. My own family doesn't support me.* His attitude was, *I can make it without their support. I can make it without their approval.*

I don't have to have their encouragement. Instead of depending on people's approval, why don't you go to God and get your approval from Him? Instead of relying on others to encourage you, start encouraging yourself. Start speaking favor, increase, healing, and destiny over your life.

If God had let the boat make it into the island bay and to anchor, it would have been so much easier. Paul and his crew wouldn't have had all the stress and trauma. They could have gotten off as if they were on a cruise and enjoyed the island. But sometimes the boat won't make it. The good news is that's not the only way to get to the shore. Paul and his crew grabbed the broken pieces from the boat, the wood that was floating, and they used that to help them swim to the shore. We think we have to have the boat, but God is so amazing that He has a plan even for the broken pieces, the remnants, the things that most people would discard. He can use them to take you where He has prepared. Their brokenness became their breakthrough.

> *Their brokenness became their breakthrough.*

Quit being discouraged over what you lost. What you have left is what you need. God didn't let you lose so much that you can't make it to where He's taking you. You didn't need the whole boat, and you have what you need. What they thought was of no use, the broken wood, was actually what they needed to make it to shore. When you're in a storm, you have to grab on to the broken pieces. That means to keep believing that you're coming out, keep declaring favor over your life, keep thanking God for His goodness. He

> *What you have left is what you need.*

didn't change His mind. The boat may have broken apart, but you're still going to stand before Caesar. What He promised is still on the way.

Get Your Passion Back

My father had a dream as a seventeen-year-old that one day he would pastor a church with thousands of people. Back in the 1930s that seemed impossible. There were very few churches that large. Against all odds, he was able to go to seminary. In the late 1950s, he was pastoring a growing, successful church. The church had almost a thousand members and had just built a big beautiful sanctuary. Everything was going great, but then a storm hit. When my sister Lisa was born with something like a form of cerebral palsy, my father began to search the Scriptures in a new way. He started speaking about how God is a healer and how we're supposed to live an abundant, victorious life. Much to his surprise, the congregation was not receptive to his new message, and after a very difficult period, he decided that he had to step down from the church. He was devastated. He had spent years pouring his heart into those people. It looked as though his dream was over. But God's ways are not our ways. That storm is not keeping you from your destiny, it's leading you to your destiny. God is directing the winds.

My parents went out and started Lakewood with a small group of people. He had lost over 90 percent of his congregation and was no longer affiliated with his denomination. He didn't have the support from his colleagues. Lifelong friends never spoke to him or my mother again. But God says you're going to make it without the support, without the people you lost, without the new building. The boat may sink, but God is still on the throne. What you lost is not as important as what you have left.

> What you lost is not as important as what you have left.

Lakewood grew and grew, just as God promised, and he pastored a church of thousands. But God did it in an unconventional way.

Suppose my father would have been bitter over the church's actions against him, or suppose he'd given up because of the bad breaks and betrayals. He would never have made it to the shore. He would never have stood before Caesar. You don't know what God is up to. The storms that none of us like are all a part of our destiny. Are you sitting on the sidelines, discouraged over what you lost, what you didn't get, what didn't work out? God is saying, "If you get your passion back, if you start believing again, you're still going to get there." Despite what you lost, despite who was against you, despite the mistakes you made, God's calling is still on your life. Your assignment is still waiting on you. New levels are still in your future.

What You Have Left Is What You Need

In the Scripture there was a young boy named Mephibosheth. He was the grandson of King Saul and the son of Jonathan. Jonathan and David were best friends. Mephibosheth was born into royalty, destined to take the throne, but life didn't turn out the way he thought. His father and grandfather were killed in a battle on the same day. When word reached his city, the nurse who took care of him picked him up and started to run out of the house, trying to hide him from the enemies that were coming. As they fled, she accidentally dropped Mephibosheth. Both of his feet were injured, and he became disabled for life. He could no longer walk. Years had passed, and instead of being in the palace, he was living in one of the poorest, most run-down cities of that day. It seemed as though it was just bad luck, just a bad break. It wasn't even his fault; somebody else dropped him. But God is not depending on what someone else does or doesn't do to get you to your destiny. People may have dropped you, but God knows how to pick you back up.

Years later, King David was thinking about how much he had loved his good friend Jonathan. He asked his men if any of Jonathan's relatives were still alive. They said, "Yes, his son is, but he's crippled and living in the slums." David said, "Go find him and bring him to me." You can imagine that when these officials from the palace started searching the slums, word quickly spread. "They're looking for Mephibosheth." When Mephibosheth heard this, he thought, *Oh no! I'm done. They finally found me.* He expected the worst, because his grandfather had spent years trying to kill David. They carried Mephibosheth to the palace, got him cleaned up, put new clothes on him, and brought him before David. Mephibosheth was afraid, not sure what was going to happen. David said, "Mephibosheth, don't worry, from now on you're going to live here in the palace with me. Every night you're going to eat dinner at my table. Not only that, I'm giving you all the land that belonged to your family."

As with Mephibosheth, it may look as if there's no way that what God promised you could still come to pass. It's been too long, you've had too many bad breaks, and the odds are against you. If Mephibosheth were here, he would tell you, "You're still going to get there." Despite what you lost, despite what wasn't fair, and despite how impossible it looks, you're going to make it without the boat. You're going to make it without what you thought you had to have—without the support, without the family, without the training. God has the right people already lined up to be good to you—people who will open doors, people who will make up for what you didn't get.

Now don't stay focused on what you've lost. What you have left is what you need. There's power in the broken pieces. It may

> *There's power in the broken pieces.*

not look like much, but when God breathes on them, you'll get to the shore. I believe and declare that you're still going to get well, you're still going to break the addiction, you're still going to pay your house off. Favor is coming, healing is coming, breakthroughs, divine connections, the fullness of your destiny.

CHAPTER TEN

Your Faith

In Mark 5, there was a lady who had a bleeding disorder for twelve years. She had gone to many doctors and spent all her money trying everything she could to get well, but nothing helped. She continued to get worse. I can imagine her family and friends comforting her, knowing she wasn't going to make it much longer. One day there was a big commotion in town. She found out that Jesus was passing through. She had heard the stories of how He had healed a crippled man, calmed the seas, opened blind eyes, and cured someone with leprosy. Something came alive inside. She thought, *He did this for other people. He can do it for me.* She could have been complaining, discouraged, and thinking, *Life's not fair. Why did this happen?* Instead she said to herself, "If I can get to Jesus and just touch the fringe of His robe, I know I'll be healed."

The problem was there was a huge crowd surrounding Jesus. Hundreds of people were packed in. It looked impossible. Most people would have given up and thought it was not meant to be. Not her. She started pushing her way through the crowd. "Excuse me, I need to get by. Pardon me, I have to get up front. I don't mean to be rude, but move out of my way." People gave her that look that says, "What is your problem, lady?" She was on a mission. She had a made-up mind. I'm sure she was weak. She had lost blood for years. She didn't feel like doing it, but she fought her way through the crowd. One version says, "She kept saying to herself, 'If I touch even His clothes, I know I will be healed.'" She was saying, "I know healing is coming. I know things are about to change in my favor. It's tough now. I'm tired, and I'm weak, but I know I'm close to my breakthrough." The reason she could keep going is she kept the right thoughts playing in her mind.

> The reason she could keep going is she kept the right thoughts playing in her mind.

She was so exhausted that I can imagine she finally fell to the ground. She had to crawl the last few feet. Just at the right time, she reached out and touched the edge of Jesus' robe. All of a sudden Jesus stopped. He looked at His disciples and asked, "Who just touched Me?" They said, "What do you mean? It's crowded, and everyone is touching You." Jesus said in effect, "No, everyone is bumping into Me, but somebody touched Me. Somebody drew the miracle-working power out of Me. They touched Me expecting things to change. They believed healing was coming, or they believed their child was going to turn around, or they believed new doors were going to open."

About that time Jesus looked at this woman. Their eyes met. She was afraid, thinking she had done something wrong. Jesus smiled and said, "Your faith has made you whole. Go in peace. You have been healed." Notice the key was her faith. It was great that her parents were praying, her friends were encouraging her, and her neighbors were believing with her. That's all good, but there's nothing more powerful than your faith. When you believe, when you live with the expectancy that things are going to change, when you keep saying to yourself, "I know the breakthrough is coming. I know healing is on the way. I know the right person is in my future. I know what God started He will finish," your faith can stop the Creator of the universe as He passes by. That's what activates His power.

You Can Activate God's Power

There were other sick people in the crowd that day. There's no doubt that when many people with needs bumped up against Jesus, nothing happened. But this lady touched Him. Are you brushing up against Him, or are you touching Him? Are you living with expectancy, knowing that He's bigger than your problems, greater than that sickness, more powerful than that addiction,

> *Are you brushing up against Him, or are you touching Him?*

or are you discouraged, thinking it will never change? God is passing by. He has all power. Don't just brush up against Him. Don't be passive and think you could never accomplish your dreams, never start your business, never meet the right person. Do as this woman did and touch Him, believe that it will happen.

When this lady was closest to her healing, the opposition was the greatest. It would have been easy if Jesus had been coming with just a few disciples. She could have gone out and touched Him without all the struggle, without the people in her way, without the heat of the day. She had to fight through the crowd. The crowd represents broken dreams, things that didn't work out, thoughts telling you, *It will never get better. You'll never meet the right person, never see the promise come to pass.* The crowd can be the negative words people have spoken over you, telling you that you're not talented enough, you can't accomplish your dream. If you're going to reach your potential, you're going to have to fight through some things. You can't have a weak, give-up, this-is-too-hard spirit. You have to be more determined than what's trying to stop you. You may get knocked down, but you have to get back up again. You have to have a made-up mind and say, "I'm not going to let my disappointments stop me. I'm not going to let the mistakes I made, the guilt and regrets, cause me to shrink back. I'm not going to let bad breaks, people who did me wrong, rejection, betrayal, or family who didn't support me cause me to get bitter and stay where I am. I'm going to fight through the crowd."

In many of the miracles Jesus performed, He laid His hands on people and they were healed. But in this case, Jesus didn't lay hands on the woman; the woman laid hands on Jesus. Are you waiting for God to lay hands on you, so to speak? "God, I'm discouraged. These problems are so big, and I don't know why these people did me wrong. God, whenever You're ready You can change things." No, why don't you lay your hands on Him? Why don't you release your faith? You can activate God's power. When you live with this expectancy, you go through the day not complaining about your problems, not discouraged by the negative report, not thinking your dreams are too big, but you're looking for God's

> *Jesus didn't lay hands on the woman; the woman laid hands on Jesus.*

goodness. You know the answer is on the way. "Lord, thank You that You're making a way. Thank You that things are turning in my favor. Thank You that You hold victory in store for the upright." When you do that, you're laying your hands on God. Your faith can initiate the healing. Your faith can be the catalyst for God to do amazing things.

Release Your Faith

In Acts 14, the apostle Paul was teaching the people when he noticed a crippled man in the crowd. This man had been that way since birth and had never walked. The Scripture says, "Paul realized the man had faith to be healed." Here the man was just sitting in the audience listening to Paul, but he must have had such anticipation on his face. Paul could see something in his expression, an expectancy that something good was about to happen, perhaps like a little child in a candy store. Paul was so impressed that he stopped his message and said, "Sir, I can see you're ready for a miracle. Stand up." The man stood up and was instantly healed. He began to walk for the first time. As this man did, we should live with this anticipation. Yes, we all have difficulties, we all have reasons to be sour, but don't let that talk you out of what God wants to do. You wouldn't be here if there wasn't something amazing in your future.

Can your faith be seen? Can anybody notice that you're expecting to go to a new level? Are you talking like it's going to happen, thinking like it's going to happen, acting like it's going to happen? God is passing by, but it won't matter if

Can your faith be seen?

you're negative. "I don't see how it can work out. I've been this way a long time. I never get any good breaks." You may brush up against Him, but you're not going to touch Him. You have to show God that you're ready to be healed, ready to be free, ready to go to a new level. There should be an expectancy that "It could happen today." You could meet the person of your dreams this week. You could see your health turn around this month. This could be your year where you go to a new level, where things fall into place, good breaks find you, promises you've been believing for a long time suddenly come to pass. "Joel, what if I believe for it and it doesn't happen?" What if you believe for it and it does happen? When you live with expectancy, where your faith can be seen in your attitude, in your expressions, in how you talk, that's going to cause God to notice you in a new way. God is always with us. He has us all in the palms of His hands. But faith is what gets His attention.

The Scripture says, "Without faith it is impossible to please God." That's a powerful principle. That means you can be obedi-

Don't let Him pass by and you just watch.

ent and have a sour attitude and limited vision and not please God. You can give, you can love, you can help the poor, and you can volunteer, which are all great things that we should do. But if you're not believing for things bigger than you can accomplish on your own, if you're not expecting difficulties to turn around, if you're not anticipating new levels, if you're not thanking God that He's opening doors you can't open and bringing promises to pass, then you're not releasing your faith. You have to stir up what God put in your heart. Don't let Him pass by and you just watch. "I wish that would happen to me. My problems are so big. I don't see how I can accomplish my dream." Why don't you touch Him? "Father, thank You that You're opening doors that no man can shut. Thank You that You're taking me where I can't go on my own. God, I don't see a way, but I know that You have a way. You're on the throne. You're bigger than what I'm facing. Lord, I believe the healing is on the way, the freedom is on the way, the right person is on the way, the abundance is on the way." That's how we touch God today, through our faith.

"Well, Joel, I'm waiting on God to do something." Maybe God is waiting on you. This lady didn't wait for Jesus to lay hands on her; she laid hands on Him. I know God has a perfect time, but the Scripture says, "Now faith is..." Faith is always in the now. The situation may not change instantly. I'm not saying it's going to happen overnight. We all have waiting periods. But our faith should stay active. This should be our normal way of life: "Lord, thank You that it's on the way. I'm looking for Your goodness and favor today, not next week, not next month, not next year." Stay in the now. Live with the anticipation that it could happen today.

Stay in Faith

For several years I had been believing for some new ways we could expand the ministry. Every day I would do as I'm asking you to do and say, "Lord, thank You that it's on the way. Thank You that You're making things happen that I couldn't make happen." I didn't see any sign of

> *How badly do you want it?*

it, but I went out each day with expectancy. I was looking for it, knowing that any moment it could happen. This went on month after month, even year after year, but no sign of it. How badly do you want it?

The lady in the Scripture waited twelve years. She was weak and tired, but she wanted it so badly that she fought her way through the crowd. Every voice told her to stay at home, that there were too many obstacles, that it wasn't worth the trouble. Her attitude was: *I've come too far to stop now. It may be uncomfortable, and I may not feel like it, but I'm going to get to Jesus.* She was small and frail, but I can see her moving large men out of the way. They looked at her like, "How did she get that kind of strength?" When God sees you doing your part, believing when you don't see any sign of it, thanking Him when you're weak, taking steps of faith when you're uncomfortable, God will give you strength beyond your natural ability. He'll help you do what you couldn't normally do.

I just kept believing, day after day, and thanking God. After three years, on a Monday, one of the things happened that I'd been believing for. I was so grateful. Then on Tuesday morning, something even more amazing happened. If that wasn't enough, on Tuesday

> *God will do things that leave your head spinning.*

evening, something bigger than the two combined, more than I could imagine, happened. It was like rapid fire—boom, boom, boom—a flood of God's goodness. That's the way God is. When you stay in faith and consistently thank Him, even when you don't see any sign, you'll come into these "suddenlies," when God not only surprises you, but exceeds your expectations. The Scripture talks about how God will do things that leave your head spinning. My head was spinning that night, in a good sense.

Maybe you've been praying, believing, expecting for a long time. Stay in faith. It's on the way. You're closer than you think. It's going to happen sooner than it seems. There's no sign of things improving, everything seems the same, but get ready. God is full of surprises. Many times He doesn't do things in a normal way, where it happens gradually. He'll do it suddenly, out of the ordinary. You didn't see it coming. It's because day after day, week after week, you kept touching Him, you kept expecting it, you kept talking like it was going to happen, and you kept thanking Him that it was on the way. Your faith is going to make you whole. Your faith is going to bring you out of debt. Your faith is going to break the addiction. Your faith is going to help you accomplish your dreams. Your faith is going to take you further than you've imagined.

I talked to a lady who started having problems with her legs. The muscles and joints were causing her great pain. It got to the point where she couldn't walk. All the doctors could do was prescribe her pain medicine. For several months she couldn't go to work, couldn't stand up, and had to stay at home and be off her feet. The prognosis wasn't good. She didn't know if she'd ever be able to walk again. One Saturday, she and her husband were at home watching our service online. After my sermon, I asked people to stand if they wanted to receive Christ. When her husband stood up, she was so surprised. She had this big smile. He looked at her and said, "Come on, honey, stand up with me." She was confused and replied, "What do you mean? I can't stand up." He said, "Sure you can." He took her by the hands and pulled her up. He held her there while I prayed. I can imagine God seeing her standing there, in pain, being held up by her husband, but determined to take a step of faith.

I ended the service by saying to write the date down, that it was going to be a new day of victory. That seed took root in her heart.

> *When God sees you releasing your faith, that gets His attention.*

She believed it was a new day. A few minutes later, while she was sitting on the couch, she felt her bones begin to crack and her muscles begin to move. She said, "I can't explain it, but something unusual was happening." Strength began to come into her legs; suddenly all the pain left. Her husband had fallen asleep, so she stood up and walked over to the bed to wake him. He couldn't believe it. The next morning she got up, and they went to church. She said, "Joel, I don't know what happened, but I've been walking normal ever since." What was that? Her faith made her whole. Just as the woman who fought her way through the crowd, when God sees you releasing your faith, that gets His attention. That's what activates His power. She could have been discouraged and told her husband, "I can't stand. Don't bother me." But as an act of faith, even though he had to hold her, she stood up. She was in effect touching the edge of His garment.

Negative Voices Will Try to Silence Your Faith

In Mark 10, there was a blind beggar named Bartimaeus sitting on the side of the road. Jesus was leaving the city of Jericho and about to pass in front of him. When Bartimaeus heard all the commotion and found out it was about Jesus, he started shouting, "Jesus, Son of David, have mercy on me!" Technically, Jesus wasn't the son of

David. He was the son of Joseph. Why did Bartimaeus call Him the son of David? He recognized Jesus as the Messiah. A few chapters earlier, the religious leaders, especially the Pharisees, didn't recognize Jesus. They thought He was a fraud, and they were jealous and intimidated. It's interesting that Bartimaeus, a man who didn't have physical sight, would clearly recognize Him as the Messiah. When he cried out "Jesus, Son of David," he was saying, "Messiah, deliverer, healer, Most High God." Jesus stopped in His tracks. I can imagine Him thinking, *Here's someone who knows who I am. Here's someone who believes I have all power, someone who's expecting My goodness.*

When Bartimaeus started shouting, people said, "Be quiet. You're making a scene, and He's going to get upset with you." People will try to talk you out of your miracle. They'll tell you all the reasons it's not going to happen, why you won't get well, why you won't accomplish your dreams, why you won't meet the right person. I can hear someone saying, "Bartimaeus, you're blind. You've been this way your whole life. Just accept it." Their problem is they don't know what God put in you. They can't hear what you hear. Negative voices will try to discourage you, but when you get quiet, you'll hear that still small voice saying, "This addiction is not your destiny; you're better than this. Living in lack, not being able to get ahead, is not your lot in life; abundance is coming. Being depressed, having no passion, and living discouraged is not who you are; freedom is coming, joy is coming, breakthroughs are coming, new levels are coming."

God whispers dreams and promises in your spirit, what you can become. The enemy will try to drown them out. He'll use people to try to discourage you. No matter how loud they are, don't let them talk you out of what God has whispered in your spirit. The Scripture talks about the secret petitions of your heart—those are the dreams God gives you at night, the promises that you haven't told anyone. It seems too far out, as though it could never happen. That's God speaking to you. His dream for your life is so much bigger than your own.

> *No matter how loud they are, don't let them talk you out of what God has whispered in your spirit.*

Throw Off the Beggar's Coat

The people saw Bartimaeus as insignificant, as unimportant, as someone who didn't matter. He was a blind beggar. They told him to be quiet, but he shouted even louder. When Jesus heard him, He stopped and said, "Let him come to Me." The Scripture says, "Bartimaeus threw off his coat..." This was significant. In those days, people who had a legitimate disability were given an official coat from the government that gave them the right to beg. The beggar's coat was valuable. It's how they made their living. On the other hand, it labeled you as a beggar in the same way we recognize people by their uniform—a police officer, a firefighter, a doctor. When you wore this beggar's coat, everywhere you went people knew that you were at a disadvantage, you weren't up to par. It gave you a right to feel sorry for yourself, a right to be depressed, a right to sit around in dysfunction.

When Bartimaeus heard Jesus say "Come," the first thing he did was throw off his coat. His attitude was: *This is a new day. I am done feeling sorry for myself. I'm done wearing this label that says disadvantaged. I'm done begging. I don't need this coat anymore.* He changed his mind-set and was saying, "I am not a victim. I am a victor. God is still on the throne. He has beauty for these ashes. He's bigger than this sickness." He got rid of his excuses. As long as you're justifying where you are, making excuses as to why you can't rise higher, why you're at a disadvantage, why you're offended, why you can't accomplish your dreams, then you'll get stuck.

I wonder how many of us are wearing that beggar's coat: "I had a bad childhood. I have a reason to be bitter. Somebody walked out of a relationship. I have a reason to be discouraged. I came down with this illness. I lost a loved one. My company didn't give me the promotion. That's why I'm sour, that's why I'm negative." Before you're going to get well, you have to take off the beggar's coat. Can I tell you that we all have a reason to feel sorry for ourselves? Everybody's been hurt, everybody's had bad breaks, and everybody's made mistakes. Take off that coat, get rid of the excuses. It may not have been fair, but God is fair. He's a God of justice. He wouldn't have allowed it if it was going to stop your purpose.

I'm all for being compassionate, loving, kind, and caring, but I don't believe in giving people the right to feel sorry for themselves. It's not because it wasn't fair, not because life hasn't thrown you a curve, but because if you keep wearing that coat, it will keep you from seeing the beauty for ashes. It will

> *Take off the self-pity, take off the hurts, take off the disappointment.*

keep you from being vindicated, promoted, restored, and healed. God wants to make the enemy pay. He wants to bring you out better. Do your part and take off the coat. Take off the self-pity, take off the hurts, take off the disappointment. You can't reach your destiny making excuses. As long as you're wearing the beggar's coat, giving yourself the right to be angry, offended, less than, or disadvantaged, it will keep you from the new levels that belong to you. When Bartimaeus left his coat, he was not only leaving his livelihood, he was leaving the negative things of the past. It was symbolic. He was leaving the hurts, leaving the bad breaks, leaving the excuses. You have to be willing to leave some things if you're going to become all you were created to be. Maybe you need to leave bitterness, leave compromise, leave a bad attitude.

Walk by Faith

Jesus called Bartimaeus to come to Him. He couldn't see, but he started walking toward Jesus based on what he heard. You may not see healing yet, but you have to go by what you've heard. "By His stripes I am healed." Business is slow. You don't see increase yet. Go by what you've heard. "I will lend and not borrow. What I touch will prosper and succeed." Your child is off course. There's no sign of things getting better. "As for me and my house, we will serve the Lord." You have to walk by faith and not by sight.

Jesus asked Bartimaeus, "What do you want Me to do for you?" He said, "Lord, I want to see." Jesus said, "Your faith has made you whole. Go in peace." Instantly he could see. God is saying to us what He said to him. Your faith is going to turn things around. Your faith is going to open the right doors. Your faith is going to bring unexpected favor. It's going to happen sooner than you think. Keep expecting it. Keep talking like it's going to happen, acting like it's going to happen, thinking like it's going to happen.

God is passing by. Don't just bump up against Him, reach out and touch Him. Release your faith. If you do this as Bartimaeus did, I believe and declare that your faith is going to take you where you couldn't go on your own. God is about to supernaturally open doors and turn impossible situations around. Your faith is going to bring freedom, promotion, breakthroughs, abundance, and the fullness of your destiny.

CHAPTER ELEVEN

A Nevertheless Person

We all face situations that seem impossible. It doesn't look as though we'll ever accomplish a dream, ever meet the right person, ever get the break we need. In the natural, we're stuck. The medical report says we're not going to get well. We raised our child in church, but now he's off course, not interested in doing right. In our career, we worked hard, took the extra training, gave it our best efforts, but now we've peaked and gone as far as our education allows. What do you do when you've done the right thing, but it hasn't worked out? You're standing on God's promises, believing that He's restoring health to you, that you'll lend and not borrow, that He'll give you the desires of your heart, but all the circumstances say just the opposite. Your reasoning, your logic says, "Forget it. It's never going to happen. This is my lot in life." It's easy to get discouraged and give up on what we're believing for.

This is where Peter was in the Scripture. In Luke 5, he and his partners had been out fishing all night and caught nothing. He was an experienced fisherman. They went to the places where there were always fish, tried again and again, hour after hour, but came up empty. They were using large nets, not fishing poles. You would have thought they would have caught something, at least a few fish, even if it was the kind they didn't want. But Peter said, "We've caught nothing." In other words, it couldn't get any worse. They came up totally empty. In the morning, as they were coming in from a long night of frustration where nothing worked out, they saw Jesus on the shore. Jesus asked if He could borrow Peter's boat, from which He would teach the large crowd of people that had gathered there. When He finished teaching, He told Peter to do something that seemed illogical. It didn't make sense to Peter's natural reasoning. He said, "Peter, go back and throw out your nets into the deep, and you'll catch a great haul of fish."

You can imagine what Peter must have thought. *Are you kidding? We've been out there fishing all night. We're the experts. We know what we're doing. There are no fish out there. Besides, it's morning now. The fish go down deeper to get out of the daylight.* Every voice told Peter, "Don't do it. It's going to be a waste of your time." If he had reasoned it out, thought about it only logically, statistically, he would have talked himself out of it. He could have told Jesus, "I appreciate Your suggestion. Thank You for Your advice, but we're not going to go back out. It's not going to do any good." Instead, Peter did something that we all must do if we're going to see promises come to pass. He said, "Master, we have worked all night and caught nothing; nevertheless, at Your word I will throw out the nets." He didn't deny the facts. He said in effect, "The odds are against us. It looks impossible. Nevertheless, because of what You say, I'm going to do it." He went back and caught so many fish that their net began to break and the catch filled their boat and their partners' boat.

Practical people would have missed their miracle. People who only look at things logically, reasonably, and statistically would have

> *Practical people would have missed their miracle.*

talked themselves out of it. God is looking for "nevertheless" people, for people who say, "The medical report doesn't look good; nevertheless, God is restoring health to me. My child is off course; nevertheless, as for me and my house we will serve the Lord. It doesn't look as though I'll ever get out of debt. The fish are not biting; nevertheless, blessings are chasing me down, and I will lend and not borrow. I've had this addiction for years, been through treatment, and nothing has worked. I could give up, but I'm a nevertheless person. I know freedom is in my future. I know one touch of God's favor can turn it around." It may not make sense in your logic. In the natural, you don't see how you could ever accomplish your dream, meet the right person, or see your family restored. You've tried your best, exhausted your resources, but you came up short. No fish. All the facts say it's never going to work out. You're right where Peter was. You can get discouraged, give up, and think it's never going to happen, or you can do as he did and say, "The odds are against me. It looks impossible. I tried and it didn't work out; nevertheless, I still believe. Nevertheless, I'm going to try again. Nevertheless, I'm going to keep praying, hoping, expecting."

Don't Stop with the Facts

If you don't learn to become a nevertheless person, you won't reach the fullness of your destiny, because there will be situations where there is no way out in the natural. The obstacle is too big, the opponents are too strong. Without God's favor, you'll get stuck. God puts us in these situations, where we come to the end of our ability, on purpose. There's nothing more we can do. This is what faith is all about. If you can accomplish it on your own, you don't need God's help. But His plan for your life is to take you further than you've imagined. That's why He puts things in your heart that are bigger than you can achieve. You don't have the talent, the resources, or the experience. Without His help, it won't happen. Too often we get discouraged and think, *This is just out of my league. This is over my head. I'll never live in a nice house. I don't have the funds. I'll never get well. I've had this sickness for years. I'll never write that book, start that business, or build that orphanage. There are too many odds against me.* You are right where you're supposed to be. God wouldn't have put that desire in you if He didn't already have a way to bring it to pass. Your attitude should be: *It looks too big; nevertheless, I know with God all things are possible. I don't have the connections; nevertheless, I have friends in high places. I tried and it didn't work out; nevertheless, what God started in my life He will finish.*

All through the Scripture, we see nevertheless people. When David went out to face Goliath, he was a teenager who'd been taking care of his father's

> *The key is that you have to add the nevertheless.*

sheep. He didn't have any military training, any experience, any armor. Goliath was twice his size, a skilled soldier. David could have looked at it in the natural and gotten depressed. But David was a nevertheless person. He thought, *All I have is a slingshot and a few stones. This giant is much bigger and much stronger; nevertheless, if God be for me, who dare be against me?* If David would have stopped with the facts, he would have talked himself out of it. The key is that you have to add the nevertheless. When the medical report says you'll never get well, you have the facts, and that's fine. I'm not asking you to deny the facts. I am asking you to add the nevertheless. "This giant is way too big; nevertheless, my God is much bigger. This medical report says I'm done; nevertheless, nothing can snatch me out of God's hands. I've been single a long time, and it doesn't look as though I'll meet the right person; nevertheless, I know a divine connection is on the way. The specialists say my husband and I aren't able to have a child; nevertheless, I know there's a baby with my name on him or her."

This is what Abraham did. God gave him the promise that he and Sarah were going to have a child. They were way too old to have a baby. Sarah had gone through the change of life. This would defy the laws of nature. In fact, when Sarah overheard the Lord tell Abraham that she would have a baby within a year, the Scripture says Sarah

> *If he had looked at it only practically, logically, reasonably, he would have given up.*

laughed. It was so far out that she thought it was funny. She said, "Oh, yeah, right! That's a good one. Abraham and I are going to have a child. I don't think so." Has God ever put something in your heart that seems so unlikely, so big, that your first thought was to laugh? He whispers in your spirit that you're going to live in a nice neighborhood, or you're going to lead your company in sales, or you're going to see your family restored, or you're going to get healthy again, or you're going to write a bestselling book. On the surface, it seems so far out that we think as Sarah did: *There's no way.* Abraham could have talked himself out of it. He could have thought, *You're right, Sarah. What was I thinking? Let me come back to reality. We're too old. It's not possible.* If he had looked at it only practically, logically, reasonably, he would have given up.

But Abraham understood this principle. He said, "Yes, we're too old. Yes, it's not possible in the natural. You've been through the change of life. I shouldn't be able to father a child." If he had stopped there, we wouldn't be talking about him today. But Abraham did something that we all must do; he added the nevertheless. "Yes, we're too old; nevertheless, God can make a way. Yes, it's impossible; nevertheless, God can do the impossible. Yes, it defies the laws of nature; nevertheless, God supersedes the laws of nature." To whatever looks impossible in your life, start adding the nevertheless. Thoughts tell you, *I'm too small to get chosen for this part; nevertheless, I know God's favor is shining down on me. I don't have the training for the promotion; nevertheless, I know God is causing me to stand out. I don't have the funds to go to college; nevertheless, I know God can open the right doors.*

Don't Have a No-Way Mentality

A young man I know wanted to play baseball in college. He grew up way out in the country. He was a star player on his high school team, but there wasn't a lot of competition in his division. Different scouts came to see him play, but they all said he wasn't big enough to play in college. He received an offer from a small private school, for which he was grateful, but he had something much bigger in his heart. He was invited to try out at a major university. He was up against other players who came from top high schools in the big cities. Those players were bigger, stronger, and had more experience. When this young man got up to hit in front of all the coaches, the pressure was on. He said, "Joel, it was like something came over me, and I felt like I was ten feet tall." He hit the ball harder, farther, and more consistently than all the top-level prospects. Out of several hundred young men who tried out that day, he was the only one chosen to make that team. He was awarded a full four-year scholarship and went on to have a great college career. The odds may be against you. You may not have the size, the strength, the talent, or the expertise, but neither did David. Don't give up on what God put in your heart. Start adding the nevertheless. "God, I don't have the size; nevertheless, I believe You'll get me to where I'm supposed to be. I don't have the experience or the training; nevertheless, I know I'm surrounded by Your favor." When you add the nevertheless, that's what allows God to do great things.

> *You're prophesying your future. If you think it's impossible, it will be impossible. God is not looking for no-way people; He's looking for nevertheless people.*

Instead of having this nevertheless mentality, too many people have a no-way mentality. "No way will I get out of debt, Joel. I'm so far down in the hole. No way will I get the promotion. No way will I meet the right person. No way will I be successful. I come from the wrong family." You're prophesying your future. If you think it's impossible, it will be impossible. God is not looking for no-way people; He's looking for nevertheless people. He's looking for people who say, "I don't see how I'll ever get out of this problem; nevertheless, God always causes me to triumph.

This legal situation looks as though it will be the end of me; nevertheless, no weapon formed against me will prosper. This dream is taking a long time; nevertheless, what God started in my life, He will finish." Get rid of the no-way mentality and switch over to a nevertheless mentality.

In the Old Testament, the Israelites were camped next door to the Promised Land. God had brought them out of slavery, opened a way through the Red Sea, and given them food and water in the desert. They had seen great miracles, and now they had finally made it to the Promised Land. Moses sent twelve men to spy out the land and see what it was like. Ten of them came back and said, "Moses, it's impossible. There are giants in the land, and the people are huge. We don't have a chance. We felt like we were grasshoppers compared to them." When they saw how big their opponents were and how impossible it looked, they made the mistake that many of us make today. They stopped right there and thought, *You can't argue with the facts. You can't deny these people are huge. They're so much bigger and stronger than us. We don't have a chance.* They looked at it only with their natural, logical reasoning, and they talked themselves out of it. They had a no-way mentality, and that generation of Israelites never did go into the Promised Land.

I wonder what would have happened if they had added the nevertheless. What if those spies had come back and said, "Moses, the people are huge. They're much bigger than us. It looks impossible; nevertheless, we are well able. Nevertheless, we are armed with strength for this battle. Nevertheless, the forces for us are greater than the forces against us." If they had had a nevertheless mentality, the same God who parted the Red Sea, the same God who brought water out of a rock, the same God who caused Pharaoh to let them go, with their Egyptian captors giving them jewels and valuables on the way out, the same God would have helped them defeat the giants. Instead of wandering around in the desert for forty years, they would have lived in the Promised Land for those forty years.

> *Instead of wandering around in the desert for forty years, they would have lived in the Promised Land for those forty years.*

Don't let a no-way mentality keep you from God's best. When it looks impossible, you don't have to deny the facts; just add the nevertheless. "These opponents are huge; nevertheless, I know that God and I are a majority. This sickness looks permanent; nevertheless, I know it's only temporary, that God is turning it around. I don't see how I could ever afford a nice house; nevertheless, I know that God has explosive blessings coming my way. It doesn't look as though we'll ever get past this loss; nevertheless, I know that God has beauty for ashes, that He can turn this mourning into dancing." Don't be a no-way person, be a nevertheless person. That means you choose to believe when the odds are against you. You stay in faith even when you don't see a way. You thank God for His goodness even though it looks impossible.

Don't Let Circumstances Talk You Out of It

A few years after Victoria and I were married, we sold our town-house and moved into a very old, run-down house close to the city. The house wasn't worth anything, but it was on a half-acre lot that was right across the street from a nice neighborhood. We would go out at night and take walks. One evening as we were walking, we came to a big two-story house that was in the final stages of construction. They were putting the finishing touches on it. Nobody was there, so we walked up to it and went inside. It was so beautiful. It had high ceilings, big tall windows, and everything was new and pristine. Here we were, living close by in a sixty-year-old house that nobody had taken care of. It was run-down, and had leaks and foundation problems. We had fixed it up enough that it was livable, but there was no comparison between our old house and this new beautiful house.

We were in awe of what we had just seen. We were in our mid-twenties at the time, and as we walked down the front sidewalk, Victoria stopped and said, "Joel, one day we're going to live in a house just like this." I looked at her as though she had lost her mind. I went on to tell her all the reasons why we weren't ever going to live in a house like that. I went down the list: "I work for a ministry, and I'll never have those kinds of funds. We can barely afford a house that's sixty years old and has crooked floors. It will take us thirty years to pay it off." I was passionate about my doubt. I wanted her to doubt with me. I went on and on and on, telling her why it wasn't going to work out. She paid no attention to me. I might as well have been talking to a tree. She said, "No, Joel, I can feel it right down in my heart. One day we're going to live in a house like that."

The difference between Victoria and me is that I saw the facts. I knew how much money we earned, I knew how impossible it was, and I let the facts talk me out of it. I had a no-way mentality. She saw the same facts, she knew our situation, but instead of focusing on the facts, she added the nevertheless. Her attitude was: *I know it's impossible now; nevertheless, with God all things are possible.* She was saying, "In the natural, it's not going to happen; nevertheless, we serve a supernatural God. He knows how to open the windows of Heaven." About a year later, that's what happened. One day a builder knocked on our door. We didn't go to him; he came to us. We sold half of our property to him for more than we had paid for the whole property. He built two new homes on it; one was for us. We ended up living in a house just like the one we had seen. Victoria barely let me come in. I almost had to live in the garage. I had a no-way mentality. Thank God that she had a nevertheless mentality.

Are you letting your circumstances talk you out of God's best? Are you talking yourself out of being healthy, being free, being prosperous, being fulfilled? "Well, Joel, I've been single a long time. I don't think I'll ever meet anyone." Get out of that no-way mentality. Turn it around. "Yes, I've been single a long time; nevertheless, I know the right person is headed my way. Somebody fine is in my future." Throw that second part in, too. On paper, it may look as though you'll never get out of debt. I'm not asking you to deny that, but add the nevertheless. "It doesn't look good on paper; nevertheless, God, I believe You have explosive blessings coming my way." Instead of just saying, "I'll never break this addiction. I've had it too long," add, "nevertheless, I know it didn't come to stay. It came to pass. Freedom, wholeness, and victory are on the way."

> *Are you talking yourself out of being healthy, being free, being prosperous, being fulfilled?*

Go Back and Try Again

What's interesting is that Peter went back to the same place where he hadn't caught any fish the whole night before and suddenly his net was filled with fish. Sometimes we think, *I've tried this once, and it didn't work out. It's never going to happen.* How do you know that God hasn't put the fish there for you now? Don't give up and quit believing. Go back and try again. God controls the whole universe. It may not have happened yet, but that doesn't mean it's not going to happen. Just as an abundance of fish was waiting for Peter, God has an abundance of what you need just waiting for you. You haven't missed it. It's not too late. If you have this nevertheless mentality, He's going to lead you into increase, into favor, into new opportunities.

A lady named Elizabeth Blackwell lived in the 1800s. She had a dream to become a medical doctor, which was unheard of back then. There were no female physicians. She applied to medical schools but was turned down twenty-nine times.

> *Just because your fish were not there last time, doesn't mean they're not going to be there this time.*

Most people would have given up and thought, *It's not meant to be. I get the message. No doors are opening,* but not Elizabeth Blackwell. She was a nevertheless person. She knew God put that dream in her heart, that He had the final say. Even though every circumstance said it was not going to happen, her attitude was: *Nevertheless, I'm going to keep trying.* She applied to school number thirty. This time the administration was faintly open to it, but they had to get the male students' approval. When all the young men were told that a female wanted to attend, they unanimously voted yes. She graduated from medical school and went on to become the first female physician in America. She started the New York Infirmary for Women and Children and later founded the London School of Medicine for Women. Just because your fish were not there last time, doesn't mean they're not going to be there this time. You have to do as Elizabeth did and say, "God, everything tells me it's over; that it doesn't make sense in the natural. I have been turned down again and again; nevertheless, at Your word I'm going to try again. I'm going to keep believing." When you're a nevertheless person, God will bring the fish to you. He'll cause doors to open. He'll put you at the right place.

David said in Psalm 3, "Lord, how are they increased that trouble me?" He was saying, "God, it looks like my enemies are multiplying." David not only had other armies trying to stop him, but his own son Absalom was coming against him and trying to take the kingdom. David could have given up and thought, *That's it. I can handle people from the outside trying to take me down, but now it's my own son. I'm done.* This could have been the point where David faded off into the sunset and we never read any more about him. But David didn't just talk about the problem. He stated the facts, but then he took it one step further. He said, "How are they increased that trouble me...but You, O Lord, are a shield for me." Notice David added the nevertheless. "I'm having a lot of trouble; nevertheless, the Lord is my shield." What's the message? Don't let the enemy have the last word. Always add the nevertheless. "The medical report doesn't look good; nevertheless, the Lord is my healer. A coworker did me wrong; nevertheless, God is fighting my battles. I went through a loss; nevertheless, God has beauty for ashes."

Some of the things that have you worried right now, things that have upset and discouraged you, would all change if you start adding the nevertheless. If you stop at the problem, at what didn't work out, at how impossible it is, that's going to keep you down. Every time something negative happens—every attack, disappointment, delay—answer back with a nevertheless. When you get stuck in traffic, just say, "I should be upset; nevertheless, I know God is directing my steps." When you have situations that look impossible, when you don't see how it could happen, don't talk yourself out of it. If you get rid of a no-way mentality and have a nevertheless mentality, God is about to turn things around. He's about to open new doors. There are explosive blessings, divine connections, and new opportunities headed your way. Because you're a nevertheless person, I believe and declare that you will see the promises come to pass as Abraham did. You will overcome obstacles that are much bigger as David did. God is going to bring the fish to you as He did to Peter, an abundance of what you need.

CHAPTER TWELVE

By This I Know

We've all come through challenges and difficulties that should have stopped us. There have been problems that seemed too big, obstacles that looked insurmountable, but somehow, we made it through. We've seen doors open that shouldn't have opened, promotion that we didn't deserve, people who for no reason went out of their way to be good to us. That wasn't luck. It wasn't just a good break. That was the hand of God pushing back forces of darkness, protecting us, healing us, promoting us. David says in Psalm 41, "By this I know the Lord is on my side, He has not let my enemies triumph over me." When David looked at where he was and thought about all he had been through to get there—the rejection, his father leaving him out, King Saul trying to kill him, people slandering him, armies coming together and attacking him—he recognized that the whole time, God was behind the scenes, fighting his battles, not letting those enemies defeat him. It gave him a boldness, a confidence. He knew the Lord was on his side.

All of us have some of these "by this I know" times. That sickness could have been the end, but by the grace of God, you're still here, healthy and whole. You can look back and say as David did, "By this I know the Lord is on my side, He didn't let that sickness defeat me." A divorce or breakup should have left you sour, bitter, and lonely. God not only restored you, but He brought somebody new, somebody better than you've imagined. Now you're happy, whole, and loving life. You can say, "By this I know the Lord is on my side, He's turned my mourning into dancing."

A young lady showed me pictures of a car she had been driving. Someone pulled in front of her on the freeway, she swerved, and her car flipped over and rolled three times. There was nothing left of her car. It didn't look as though there was any way someone could survive. She said, "Joel, I walked away without one scratch, without one bruise." The police couldn't believe it. When they saw the car, they were expecting a fatality. They had to use the Jaws of Life to pull her out. One officer said, "You are one very lucky lady." That's not luck; that's the hand of God. Those were angels watching over her, keeping her from dashing her foot against a stone. She can look back and say, "By this I know the Lord is on my side."

> *That's not luck; that's the hand of God.*

Fuel for Your Faith

There are things that should have stopped you—the people who were against you, the rejection, the bad childhood, the addiction. Other people were defeated by those things; other people got knocked down and didn't get up. But look at you. You're still standing. You're still blessed, you're still happy, and you're still victorious. That's a sign the Lord is on your side. Just the fact that you're here is a sign. If some people had gone through what you've been through, they wouldn't have made it. Look back at how you outlasted the opposition, how you raised that child on your own, how you put yourself through college, how you came out of dysfunction, or how you made it through the treatment. Other people would have given up. Other people would have complained, gotten bitter, and missed their destiny. But by the grace of God, here you are. When you know the Lord is on your side, it gives you a confidence, a boldness. You don't fall apart when opposition comes. Your attitude is: *You're messing with the wrong person. I may look ordinary, but I have a secret: The Most High God, the Creator of the universe, is on my side.*

How do you know that? He didn't let your enemies triumph over you. You didn't make it through that problem on your own. That was God fighting your battles. You didn't break the addiction by yourself. You did your part, but that was God keeping it from stopping your purpose. You didn't meet the person you fell in love with by accident. It wasn't a coincidence that she crossed your path. She could have been five minutes later, and you'd never have seen her. He could have changed his mind and gone somewhere else that day, but God ordered his steps, and now you're blessed with somebody to love.

Every challenge God has brought you through into victory was designed as fuel for your faith. It's so that when you face new challenges, you can look back and say, "God, You did it for me back then, and I know You'll do it for me now." You have a history with God. You've

> You have a history with God.

seen Him make a way where you didn't see a way. You've seen Him have you at the right place at the right time, and you met someone who was instrumental in your destiny. You've seen Him show you mercy when you made a mistake and turn it around even though you didn't deserve it. In big and small ways, we've all seen the hand of God. When you're tempted to get discouraged and think, *This problem is too big. It will never change. I'll never get promoted. I'll never break this addiction*, you need to go back and get some fuel. Remember what God has done. Think about the times He's shown out in your life.

Go back over your history and see how God has never left you, how He kept you from that accident, brought the right person, or led you to the house where things fell into place. Then when thoughts whisper, *It's never going to happen. This is as good as it gets*, just smile and say, "I'm sorry, but you're too late. I have a history with God. I've already seen His goodness. I've already seen Him turn my child around. I've seen Him heal my loved one. I've seen Him promote me when others were trying to push me down. I've seen Him bring me through the loss and give me beauty for ashes." When you look back at your history, it will give you fuel for your destiny.

He Will Make Your Mission Successful

In Genesis 24, Abraham was old and close to death. He told his assistant to travel back to his hometown to find his son Isaac a wife. They were living in Canaan, but Abraham wanted Isaac to marry someone from his original home. Abraham was very wealthy, and he was going to leave everything to Isaac. The assistant felt all this pressure. He thought, *How am I going to know if it's the right girl?* He said to Abraham, "I'll go, but what if I don't find a young woman who will come back with me?" Abraham said, "You will, for the Lord, in whose presence I have walked, will send His angel with you and make your mission successful." Abraham was saying, "Don't worry. I have a history with God. I've seen His faithfulness down through the years. He gave us a child whom He promised even though we were way too old. He provided a ram in the bush when I thought I was going to have to sacrifice my son. He showed me mercy when I made a mistake and had a baby out of wedlock. He rescued my nephew Lot when he was in trouble." He had seen God's goodness again and again. He had such confidence that he could say with boldness, "It will happen. I have walked with God."

When you look back over your life as Abraham did, you'll see times when God brought a promise to pass that looked impossible. He provided when you didn't see a way. He showed you mercy and turned a situation around. He brought a child out of trouble, and now they're doing great things. When you think about the faithfulness of God, you'll have the confidence to say, "It will happen. My children will be mighty in the land. I will live and not die. I will lend and not borrow. I will break this addiction. I will accomplish my dreams. I will reach my destiny." How can you be so sure? You have a history with God. Look back at what He's done. You didn't get here by yourself. God was directing your steps. Behind the scenes, you couldn't see it but He was pushing back the opposition, He was favoring you, He was dealing with

> *Look back at what He's done. You didn't get here by yourself.*

those enemies. That's why they couldn't defeat you. That's why you had the baby when the experts said you couldn't. That's why they called you and offered you the promotion. You didn't go after it; it came after you. That's wasn't good luck; that was a good God.

Instead of wondering if it's going to work out, worrying about your health, stressing over your finances, have a new attitude: *The Lord in whose presence I have walked, the Lord who has defeated my enemies, the Lord who has restored and vindicated me, the Lord who has promoted and prospered me will make my mission successful.* God has not brought you this far to leave you. He defeated enemies for you in the past, and the good news is that He's still on the throne and He's going to do it again in the future.

Think about all the circumstances that could have brought you down, but you're still going strong. Look at all the people who could have held you back. They told you what you couldn't do, tried to discredit you and make you look bad, but you just kept on keeping on, and today you're still going strong and they're nowhere to be found. By this you can know the Lord is on your side, He didn't let them defeat you. You could have been discouraged, you could have believed what they said, but He didn't let their negative words stick. He didn't let their prophecy come to pass. He spoke new words into your spirit. He said, "No weapon formed against you is going to prosper." He said, "When your enemies come against you one way, I will defeat them and cause them to flee seven different ways." He said, "When opposition tries to stop you, I will raise up a barrier."

You Have a Protector and Guardian

When we were trying to acquire the Compaq Center, the company we were up against was one of the largest taxpayers in Texas. It was David versus Goliath. In the natural, we didn't have a chance. The odds were against us. But I've learned that you and God are a majority. He can make things happen that you could never make happen. We needed ten votes from the Houston city council members, but we only had nine. The night before the main vote, a young Jewish council member who had been against us for two years changed his mind and decided to vote for us. We got the Compaq Center. We were so thrilled. I asked the council member what happened. He told how he received a phone call from an older Jewish lady whom he hadn't spoken to in over twenty years, but he always had great respect for her. She told him in no uncertain terms that he was to vote for Lakewood. That lady whom I had never met changed his mind. I couldn't have made that happen.

Every time I see our facility I can say, "By this I know the Lord is on my side, He didn't let those enemies defeat us." Our building is a sign of God's goodness. It's a reminder that He's fighting our battles, that He's bigger than what we're facing. Look back over your life and remember what God has done for you. That's fuel for your faith. You have a history with God. Sometimes we forget the good things, and we remember the hurts, the disappointments, and the mistakes. But look where you are now. If it had not been for the goodness of God, you wouldn't be here.

> *There are enemies you never saw that God kept out of your path.*

Some people who went through what you went through didn't make it. They got depressed, they gave up, they're living defeated, but not you. God shined His favor on you. He's been keeping enemies from defeating you for your whole life. He was protecting you and guarding you even when you didn't realize it. There are enemies you never saw that God kept out of your path.

In Chapter Five, I told how when my father was a little boy, he fell into a fire and could have easily been killed. Another few seconds and he wouldn't have made it. Somebody just happened to be right there to pull him out. The enemy has been trying to take you out since you were a baby. It's because he knows you're a person of destiny. He knows you have seeds of greatness. He knows you've been crowned with favor, so he's been working overtime trying to silence your voice, stop your gifts, limit your potential, and keep you from leaving your mark. But those forces have not been able to stop you. It's because you have a protector, a defender, who's been watching over you. He never sleeps. He's pushing back the darkness, keeping those forces from taking your life. David says, "A thousand may fall at your side, and ten thousand at your right hand, but it will not come near you." God has His angels standing guard over you. The fact that you're here, alive and victorious—by this you can know the Lord is on your side.

When I see my mother, still alive and healthy forty years after her cancer diagnosis, by this I know the Lord is on my side. He didn't let that sickness take her life. I never dreamed I could step up to minister. I didn't have the experience or the training, but God brought gifts out of me that I didn't know I had. He's promoted me, taken me where I couldn't go on my own, caused me to outlast the opposition. By this I know the Lord is on my side, my enemies could not defeat me. When I look at Victoria and see how beautiful she is, by this I know the Lord is on my side. The Scripture says, "Taste and see that the Lord is good." I don't know about you, but I have tasted God's goodness. I've seen His favor, His blessing, His healing, His vindication, and His abundance. When you look at where you are and think about what it took to get you there, that's fuel for your faith.

Go Back over Your History

In that battle for the Compaq Center, there were a few high-powered people who didn't want us to have it. One of the main business leaders, a very influential man, was at a luncheon with some local business executives, including a friend of mine. He told the whole group at their table, "It will be a cold day in Hell before Lakewood gets the Compaq Center." He said it very

> *"It will be a cold day in Hell before Lakewood gets the Compaq Center."*

sarcastically, and some of the others laughed. He didn't know the one man was my friend. When my friend told me what the man said, it didn't discourage me. It did just the opposite; it made me more determined. I prayed harder, and I stood stronger. You can't have a big testimony without a big test. Sometimes God will send a big enemy. Stay in faith. They can't stop your destiny. They don't know it, but God is going to use them for fuel. I can imagine now that every time that man drives by our building, every time he flips through the channels and sees my smiling face, he must think that it's a cold day in Hell because there we are. He went from being opposition to being fuel. Now when I face other giants, I think about him. He couldn't stop us. He thought we were a lightweight. What he couldn't see was that behind the scenes, we had a heavyweight, the Most High God, fighting our battles.

When I'm tempted to get discouraged, I go back over my history. God brought my father out of poverty. He was the first one in his family to give his life to Christ. That wasn't a lucky break. That was God choosing my father before he could choose Him. If it was not for God's goodness in my father's life, I wouldn't be here.

I think about how God protected me on the freeway when I lost control of my car during a big rainstorm. I hit the guardrail in the center and started spinning around and around, crossing five lanes of traffic. At one point I was facing the wrong way, and an eighteen-wheeler was coming right at me. We were so close I felt as though I could touch his front grille. It was all in slow motion. I had time to think, *This is it*. All I could say was "Jesus." The Scripture says to call on the name of the Lord and you will be saved. It doesn't say you have to pray long, because Heaven and Earth come to attention when you say "Jesus." The next thing I knew I was stopped on the side of the freeway. The eighteen-wheeler pulled over, and the driver got out and came to my window. He said, "Boy, you must be living right. Just when I was about to hit you, a big gust of wind blew my truck into the next lane and somehow I missed you." He said "somehow"; I realize it was Someone. He thought I was lucky; I know it was the goodness of God. By this I know the Lord is on my side: He didn't let that accident take my life.

What has God done for you? You have some of these "by this I know" times. Those victories weren't just to protect you, to promote you, to heal you. They're fuel. When you face new challenges, when obstacles look too big, if you remember what God has done, that's what gives you the faith, the confidence, the knowing that He's in control, that He has you in the palms of His hands, that what's trying to stop you doesn't have a chance. The enemy may do his best, but his best will never be enough. The forces for you are greater than the forces against you. Don't live worried or afraid. Go back over your history. When you start thanking God, faith will rise in your heart. You'll know that God did it for you back then, and He'll do it for you today.

> *What has God done for you? You have some of these "by this I know" times.*

Never Forget the Amazing Things

This is where the Israelites missed it. God supernaturally brought them out of slavery in Egypt. When He sent plagues on their enemies, they were living next door, but the plagues never affected the Israelites. When Pharaoh changed his mind and came chasing after them, they were at a dead end at the Red Sea. It looked as though they were done, but God parted the sea and they went through on dry ground. When Pharaoh's army tried to go through, they were all drowned. Out in the desert, God brought the Israelites water out of a rock and gave them manna each morning to eat. It was one miracle after another. But when they arrived at the Promised Land and saw how big the inhabitants were, instead of using what God had done for them as fuel, instead of saying "by this we know the Lord is on our side," Psalm 78 says, "They forgot the amazing miracles God had done." They got discouraged and started complaining and saying, "Moses, we don't have a chance. We'll never defeat them. Let's go back to being slaves." Here they had a great history with God. He had done amazing things, but their problem was that they didn't remember them. Instead of going into the Promised Land, they ended up wandering in the desert for forty years.

Are you living worried, thinking a problem is too big? Are you discouraged by a medical report, stressed out over a financial situation? Perhaps you've done as the Israelites did, and you've forgotten what God has done. You're out of fuel; your faith needs to be reenergized. The way you do this is by going back over your "by this I know" moments.

> *It's great that David defeated Goliath, but what about the giants that you've defeated?*

Remember the times God made a way, the times He delivered you, opened that door you couldn't open, and protected you. You need to start dwelling on the goodness of God in your own life, not what He did for your neighbor. It's great that He parted the Red Sea for the Israelites, but how about the Red Seas that He's parted for you? It's great that David defeated Goliath, but what about the giants that you've defeated? It's great we're in the Compaq Center, but what about the Compaq Centers that God has given you? What about the times He made something happen that seemed impossible? Your personal history is your fuel. When you start thanking God for those things, you'll get that spring back in your step. You'll live with the confidence that says "by this I know the Lord is on my side."

I talked to a man who struggled with addictions for twenty-seven years. He was an executive who had had a great job and a happy family, but drugs and alcohol ruined his life. He lost his marriage and his job. He was so depressed that he didn't want to live. At his lowest point, he turned the television on and there I was talking about how God is bigger than any addiction, how one touch of His favor can turn things around, how you're never too far gone. All of a sudden he felt a warmth starting at his head and flowing down to his feet. He said, "For the first time in years, I felt hopeful, as though I could get back to where I was supposed to be." He got down on his knees and said, "God, I can't do this on my own. Help me to change." That night was a turning point. Those chains were broken off him. That was over ten years ago and he's been sober ever since. He never touched alcohol again. He never went back to drugs. What he couldn't do on his own for years, God did in a split second. He and his wife had divorced, but they remarried and he's back with his family.

Now he can say, as David did, "By this I *know* the Lord is on my side"—not I think, not I hope, not I'm believing, not I'm praying. God is going to do some things in your life where you know He's on your side. There will be no doubt. As with him, you couldn't break an addiction, but suddenly you're free. You were told you couldn't have children, but now you have a healthy baby. You weren't even looking, yet somebody amazing came into your life. The opposition was much bigger and stronger, but the Compaq Center came to you, the promotion came to you, the house came to you, the business came to you, the movie came to you. You couldn't have made it happen.

> *What He's done in the past is going to pale in comparison to what He's about to do.*

You were at your limits, but the Red Sea parted. Get ready. You're about to know the Lord is on your side. What He's done in the past is going to pale in comparison to what He's about to do.

Now don't be surprised when you face giants bigger than you've ever seen. Bigger opposition is a sign you're headed to a new level. You'll be tempted to worry, to feel overwhelmed, but you have to go back and get your fuel. Remember what God has done. Thank Him for the Red Seas He's parted. Thank Him for the giants you've defeated. Thank Him for the times He made a way. There are things that should have stopped you. You can say with David, "By this I know the Lord is on my side. The cancer didn't defeat me. The bad childhood didn't limit me. The accident didn't take my life. The divorce didn't keep me from my destiny." You have a history with God. He's brought you through in the past, and He's going to bring you through in the future. He was fighting your battles then, and He's fighting your battles now. I believe and declare you're about to take new ground, you're going to go where no one in your family has gone. Giants that are much bigger are about to come down. God is going to show out in your life in a greater way. By this you will know the Lord is on your side.

CHAPTER THIRTEEN

The Hot Winds of Testing

We all go through seasons in life that are difficult. We're going along fine, and then an unexpected challenge comes. We're diagnosed with an illness, our child is in trouble, the pandemic hits, our business slows down. It's easy to get discouraged and wonder why it happened. But God doesn't stop every difficulty. He will allow challenges to move us into our purpose. If you pass the test, on the other side of that difficulty is a new level of your destiny. Jesus told a parable in Luke 8 about a farmer who sowed seed in his land. Some seed fell on good ground; some fell on hard ground.

> How you respond in these difficult times will determine whether you come out bitter or you come out better.

When He explained the meaning, He said, "The seeds in the rocky soil become like young plants whose roots don't go down very deep. They believe for a while, then they wilt when the hot winds of testing come."

You can't become who you were created to be without going through hot winds of testing. How you respond in these difficult times will determine whether you come out bitter or you come out better. These are the times when you feel overwhelmed—you're doing the right thing, but it's not improving; you're praying, but it feels like God went on vacation; you lost a loved one, and you don't see how you can make it. Those are not just random challenges or just bad luck. You're in the hot winds of testing.

God is seeing what you're made of. How deep do your roots go down? Are you going to live sour and discouraged, or are you going to dig down deep and say, "God, I may not understand it, but I trust You. I know You're bigger than what I'm facing. Your plans for me are for good. So, Lord, I thank You that You'll get me to where I'm supposed to be." You have to be determined. You're not going to be moved by what's not fair. You're not going to get bitter over who did you wrong. You're not going to live discouraged because of a bad break, a delay, or an unexpected challenge.

You may be in the hot winds of testing now. Perhaps you're dealing with an issue in your family, or at the office a coworker is leaving you out and getting on your nerves—not once, but this has gone on month after month. If your roots don't go down deep, if you live shallow, let it frustrate you, and try to pay them back, you'll get stuck where you are. That difficulty is not there to defeat you; it's there to promote you. If you pass the test, keep doing the right thing, keep being good to people, and keep letting God fight your battles, because your roots go down deep, God will not only turn it around, but He'll bring you out better. Don't let the hot winds of testing cause you to fall apart. It may be taking longer than you thought. You were determined at first, you stood strong, but now it's been a long time and you're tired. Thoughts are telling you, *It's never going to work out. You'll never get well. You'll never see*

your family restored. Don't believe those lies. That test is not permanent. God has already set an end to the difficulty. You have to get
your second wind. God didn't bring you this far to leave you. What
He started He's going to finish. Dig down deep and keep passing
the test. Keep thanking Him that it's on the way. Keep declaring
what He promised. Keep believing when you don't see any sign of
it. Stay in this attitude of faith.

Just Stand

"Well, Joel, I don't understand why this happened. I was being my
best. Why did I have this bad break? Why did I come down with this
illness? Why did these people turn on me?" It's just life. Being persons
of faith doesn't exempt us from difficulty. These tests come to us all.
The apostle Paul says in Ephesians, "Put on the whole armor of God,
so in the evil day, you will be able to stand, and having done all, to
stand." He didn't say to do this just in case you have an evil day, or
maybe you'll have some trouble. He said to put the armor on "so in
the evil day." He was saying that there's going to be some hot winds
of testing. You're going to have things in life that can knock the wind
out of you, take your joy, and cause you to give up on your dreams.
If you're going to pass the test, your roots have to go down deep. You
can't be weak and complain, "God, why did this happen?" You have
to have a made-up mind that says, "I know that God is still on the
throne. I know that His being for me is more than the world being
against me. I'm not moved by what's not improving. I'm not moved
by how unfair it is. I'm not moved by what I don't understand. I know
that what was meant for harm, God is turning to my advantage."

Paul said that when you've done everything you know to do, just stand. You don't have to figure it out, you don't have to make things happen, and you don't have to worry. Just stand in the face of the opposition, stand when every voice says it's not going to work out, stand when the medical report is not changing,

> *If you stand immovable and unshakable, you will be unstoppable.*

stand when your finances aren't improving, and stand when your child is not making good decisions. To stand means you're not moved by what's not changing. You're not complaining because it's taking so long, you're not bitter because you had the setback, and you're not frustrated because your plans didn't work out. You are steadfast, immovable, unshakable. Your roots go down deep. You have a report of victory when you could be complaining. You talk about health when you're fighting the illness. You talk about abundance when your business is down. You talk about overcoming when you feel overcome. That's what it means to stand. You stand believing, stand trusting, stand hoping, stand expecting. If you stand immovable and unshakable, you will be unstoppable. Those hot winds of testing will not keep you from your destiny; they will launch you into your destiny.

God is not necessarily looking for people who have great faith, but for people who will simply stand. For people who stand in the middle of a pandemic and are not bitter or discouraged, but who stand with an attitude of faith. He is looking for you to stand when the problem is not turning around, stand when it's taking longer than you thought, stand when your heart is breaking, and stand when the bottom falls out. God never said we wouldn't have an evil day, a time of trouble. But He did promise that if you just stand,

He'll bring you out. If you stand, He'll defeat your enemies. If you stand, He'll give you beauty for ashes. If you stand, joy is coming in the morning. If you stand, the enemies you see today you will see no more. Don't let those hot winds of testing cause you to wilt and think, *God is not for me. I must have done something wrong.* No, you probably did something right. That's why the enemy is trying to stop you. He thought you would fall apart, get bitter, and blame God. What he didn't realize is that you know how to stand. You're not moved by the hot winds. You're not worried about the medical report or frustrated over how long it's been. You're steadfast. You're immovable.

Can I tell you that the enemy cannot defeat a stander? He can't defeat you when you stand in praise, when you thank God even when it's not working out. You stand in excellence. You keep being your best in the middle of the trouble. You stand in faith. You could be negative and sour, but you still believe God is working, and you still expect things to change. You still have your hopes up, knowing that it could turn around today. I'm not asking you to have great faith, and I'm not asking you to figure out a solution. I'm simply asking you to stand. Stand unmoved by what you're up against, stand with your eyes on the God who created the universe, knowing that He has the final say, that He's working behind the scenes, and that what He promised you will come to pass.

Are you in those hot winds, facing difficulties that seem too big? You never dreamed you would be up against this sickness, never thought your marriage would be in trouble, or never thought that company wouldn't need you. God is saying, "Stand. I'm still in control. It's not a surprise to Me." He already has the solution. He's already lined up the right people. The healing, the promotion, the breakthroughs are already en route. Here's what I've learned. I know that God is on my side not by the storms He's stopped, but by the storms that didn't stop me. You can't judge God's favor by the storms He kept you out of, but by the storms He brought you through. As we saw in the previous chapter, David said, "By this I know the Lord is on my side, He has not let my enemies

> *You can't judge God's favor by the storms He kept you out of, but by the storms He brought you through.*

triumph over me." He was saying, "I know God is on my side, because in those hot winds of testing I just kept standing and doing the right thing, and God defeated my enemies for me." The Scripture says, "You will go through the fire and not be burned, you will go through the waters and not drown, and you will go through the famine and not go hungry." Don't get discouraged over what God is bringing you through. He won't allow you to get in a difficulty that He can't bring you out of.

Let Your Roots Go Deep

In Chapter Two, I wrote about the three Hebrew teenagers who wouldn't bow down to the king's golden idol. He was so upset that he was going to have them thrown into a fiery furnace. Talk about the hot winds of testing. What they were up against seemed impossible. They could have panicked, fallen apart, and said, "God, we were being our best, doing the right thing. Why did this happen?" It's a test. God allowed the difficulty not to defeat them but to establish them. They said, "King, we're not going to bow down.

We know our God will deliver us." If they would have stopped there, we would think, *That's great. They had faith. They believed.* But what they said next shows us their real attitude. They said, "We know God will deliver us, but even if He doesn't, we're still not going to bow down." That's what it means to stand. You have a made-up mind. You're going to stay in faith whether it works out your way or not. You're going to trust God whether the door opens or closes. You're going to give Him praise whether He turns it around in five days or five years. Your roots go down deep.

You're not moved by people trying to talk you out of it. "I don't think you'll ever get well. My cousin died of that same thing." When you know how to stand, you let that go in one ear and out the other. You're not moved by opposition, by bad breaks, or by people who are not for you. You have an attitude like those teenagers: *I know God is going to turn it around, but even if He doesn't, I'm not going to live sour. I'm not going to give up on life. I'm not going to quit believing.* When you have these deep roots, the hot winds of testing don't affect you. You're stable, consistent, and unmoved. You know no weapon formed against you is going to prosper. You know all things are working together for your good.

When the king had the teenagers thrown into the furnace, it was so hot the guards who threw them in were instantly killed. The young men should have been gone, that should have ended their lives, but God has the final say over your life. No person, no bad break, no sickness, no addiction, and no disappointment can stop your purpose. When the king looked into the furnace opening and saw that they were all still alive, he couldn't believe it. Not only were they alive and loosed from their bonds, but he saw a fourth man whom he said "looks like the Son of God." Those teenagers came out unharmed, without even the smell of smoke on them.

Sometimes God will keep you out of the fire. At other times, He'll make you fireproof and send you into the furnace. You may be in the fire now and are feeling those hot winds of testing. You need to remind yourself as those teenagers did that the flames can't harm you, that trouble can't take you out, that those people can't stop what God has ordained. It's a test. Are you going to stand despite the opposition? Are you going to stay in faith despite things not working out? Are you going to keep believing even though you've had setbacks? When you can say as they did, "Even if God doesn't do it my way, I'm still not going to bow down. I'm still not going to live defeated. I'm still not going to give up on my dreams," God will make things happen that you couldn't make happen. When your roots go down deep, you'll defeat giants that are much bigger, accomplish dreams that seem impossible.

There are times in life when we all get thrown into the furnace, so to speak. We're praying, "God, keep us out, keep me from the trouble, keep me from the sickness." But here's the key: God controls the thermostat. He won't let the fire get too hot for you. He knows how much you can handle. If it feels like too much, that's because you are stronger than you think. It's because your destiny is greater than you think. God is getting you prepared for things much bigger in your future—for favor, influence, and opportunity that you've never seen. Don't wilt in the trouble. Dig down deep. It's not too much for you. You can handle it. You've been armed with strength for this battle. You are full of can-do power. The forces for you are greater than the forces against you.

You're Being Prepared for Promotion

None of us like the hot winds of testing. It would be much easier if things fell into place and we never had opposition, if people were always for us. But without these times of testing when you have to resist the urge to quit, when you have to stretch your faith and believe that God is in control, we wouldn't become who we were created to be.

I read about a team of scientists who created a miniature version of our planet that was called the Biosphere 2 Project. It's a big dome structure that cost $150 million. They made it to study how the Earth functions and to learn more about how we can make improvements. It had 3,800 species of plants and animals, including a rainforest, a savanna, and a desert. They discovered that trees in this biosphere grew much faster than trees outside the dome. But they were surprised that before these trees reached their full height, they fell over. They realized the trees couldn't withstand their own weight because they hadn't replicated the wind within the biosphere. It was always calm and peaceful. There were never any strong winds or storms. Because the trees didn't have to withstand any pressure from wind, their roots didn't develop properly. They had a deficiency in what they call "stress wood," which helps the tree grow stronger and more solidly. Without it, the trees can grow fast, but they can't survive. The wind is essential for a tree to flourish and become what it was created to be.

In the same way, without these hot winds of testing, without storms, without difficulties, our lives would be easier, but we wouldn't develop properly. We wouldn't be able to carry the weight of what God has in store. Don't complain about the wind; it's strengthening you. Those hot winds of testing can be uncomfort-able, and we don't like it, but our roots are going down deeper. You're developing courage, strength, and fortitude. Those winds are not there to break you; they're there to make you. They're helping you become who you were created to be. When you have the right perspective, you don't get discouraged when you face

> *Without these hot winds of testing, without storms, without difficulties, our lives would be easier, but we wouldn't develop properly.*

challenges. If God had left you in that biosphere, without difficul-ties, without opposition, you may have grown fast but you wouldn't have the strength for where you're going. Those hot winds of test-ing are preparing you. Every day you stand, your roots are getting stronger. Every time you praise when you could complain, you're developing stress wood. When you keep doing the right thing when the wrong thing is happening, your core is getting strength-ened to carry the weight of the blessing, the weight of the influ-ence, the weight of the anointing.

It's interesting that airplanes don't take off with the wind; they take off against the wind. The airplane needs the resistance of the wind to get lift. Are you complaining about winds being against you, when in fact God is going to use those winds to give you lift? That challenge may look like it's going to stop you, but it's really going to promote you. Don't get discouraged because you're in the hot winds of testing—that tells me you're about to lift off. You're about to see things you've never seen and go places you've never gone. Pass the test. Keep standing. Keep doing the right thing.

This is what David did. After David defeated Goliath, King Saul asked him to come to the palace and be one of his armor-

> *When you study the heroes of faith, one thing you'll find is they all went through these hot winds of testing.*

bearers. When Saul wasn't feeling well, he would have David come in and play the harp. David was faithful. He served Saul with excellence, always gave it his best, but Saul was jealous of David. He didn't like the fact that David was getting all the

people's recognition as a great warrior. One day while David was playing the harp, Saul threw a spear at him, trying to kill him, and barely missed. David had to flee for his life. He spent years in the desert on the run from King Saul. Here David hadn't done anything wrong. He could have said, "God, this isn't fair. Where are You?" But in those hot winds of testing, David kept doing the right thing. He had a chance to kill Saul, to get revenge, but he wouldn't do it. He knew Saul was anointed to be king, and David wouldn't touch God's anointed. As David kept passing the test, his roots were going down deeper, his character was being developed, he was showing God what he was made of. That's what prepared him to take the throne and do great things. When you study the heroes of faith, one thing you'll find is they all went through these hot winds of testing.

When the Israelites were in slavery, God told Moses to go and tell Pharaoh to let the people go. Moses obeyed and went, but Pharaoh said no. What do you do when you do what God tells you, but it doesn't work? You pray, you believe, you're good to people, you take the high road, but nothing's improving. Moses could have been sour and thought, *God, I did my part. I got my courage up, but it didn't happen.* Instead, he went back and told Pharaoh the same thing again and again and again. He was in the hot winds of testing. Was he going to get discouraged and give up because it wasn't happening the way he thought? Maybe you've been doing the right thing again and again, but people aren't changing, or the medical report is not improving, or your business is not getting better. This is when you have to have deep roots. "God, I'm not moved by what's not changing. I'm not discouraged by what's not happening. I'm not going to wilt, start complaining, and give up on my dreams. I'm going to keep standing. I'm going to keep doing the right thing." When you pass the test like that, instead of those winds stopping you, they will lift you; instead of defeating you, they will promote you.

Your Ninth Hour Is on the Way

Even Jesus had to go through these hot winds of testing. You would think He would have had it easy. God would surely favor Him and keep Him from opposition and bad breaks. But Jesus had to pass these same tests. People whom He loved walked away. Peter denied Him. Thomas doubted Him. The religious leaders made fun of Him. In the Garden of Gethsemane, He was so overcome with despair that His sweat was like great drops of blood. When He was crucified, the Scripture says, "Darkness fell across the whole land from the sixth to the ninth hour." As He hung there, the sun refused to shine. It was a dark moment. Jesus could have called down angels to rescue Him. He could have called down fire from Heaven, but in the dark moment He didn't take the easy way out. In the dark moment He didn't come down off the cross. Yes, He's the Son of God, but He still felt the pain. He was in so much agony that He cried out, "My God, My God, why have You forsaken Me?"

The Scripture says, "He endured the pain of the cross, looking forward to the joy that was coming." He knew that on the other side of the dark moment was a resurrection. We would never have salvation without a dark moment. Jesus would never have sat at the right hand of the Father without a dark moment.

> *We would never have salvation without a dark moment.*

Joseph would never have become the prince of Egypt without a dark moment, his brothers betraying him. Paul would never have written nearly half of the books of the New Testament without a dark moment, being imprisoned for sharing his faith. Sarah would never have given birth to the promised child without a dark moment, being barren for ninety years. When you're in a dark moment, you have to remind yourself that the difficulty is not the end; it's leading you to a resurrection, to a new beginning, to something that you've never seen. Don't give up in the dark moment. Don't quit believing in the dark moment. Don't stop doing the right thing in the dark moment.

You may feel as though God has forgotten about you. Even Jesus asked why He was forsaken. Sometimes during the test, the Teacher is silent. You don't hear anything. You don't see anything improving. But you have to know that in the dark moments God still has you in the palms of His hands. He knows it's difficult. He knows you feel overwhelmed. He knows you don't think you can go on. Don't worry. Help is on the way. Weeping endures for a night, but joy is coming in the morning. Now keep standing. Live one day at a time. Don't worry about tomorrow. You don't have grace for tomorrow. Stand today, and when you get to tomorrow, you'll have grace for that day.

It's significant that the Scripture tells us darkness covered the Earth from the sixth to the ninth hour during Jesus' crucifixion. The writer wasn't just giving us a time frame so we would know chronologically when it all happened. God was showing us that just as He sets a time for you to come into that dark moment, He sets a time for you to come out of it. Can I tell you that your ninth hour is coming? The dark moments are not permanent. The hot winds of testing don't last forever. You are close to seeing things turn around. You are close to a breakthrough, close to your healing, close to meeting the right person, close to victory like you've never seen.

The Scripture says, "The suffering of this present time doesn't compare to the glory that's coming." If you could see what God has coming—the promotion, the favor, the influence—you wouldn't complain about that dark time. You would do as Jesus did and endure a little bit longer. Keep standing. Keep honoring God. Keep being good to people. Your ninth hour is on the way. Things are about to change in your favor. The light is about to come bursting in. It's going to happen suddenly. Just as that challenge came unexpectedly, God's favor is going to show up unexpectedly. He's already set an end to the difficulty. I believe and declare you are coming into your ninth hour. That darkness is about to lift, and the hot winds of testing are about to subside. I speak strength into you, healing, favor, promotion, the fullness of your destiny.

CHAPTER FOURTEEN

Keep on Walking

We all have things we're believing for, dreams to come to pass, problems to turn around. We have the promise in our heart, but nothing is happening. We've prayed, we've believed, but we don't see any sign of things improving. It's easy to get discouraged and think it's never going to work out. But most of the time God doesn't do things instantly. There will be a waiting period. Thoughts will tell you, *It's too late. If it were going to happen, it would have happened by now.* Just because you don't see it changing doesn't mean that God is not working. As you keep believing, keep praising, keep doing the right thing, you're going to see things begin to change. Many times, the miracle is in the process. It happens when you keep being obedient. Don't be frustrated because you're not seeing immediate results. What you're believing for is still on the way.

In Luke 17, when Jesus was on His way to Jerusalem, He entered a village. He was met by ten lepers who began to shout, "Jesus, have mercy on us and heal us!" Jesus could have gone over and healed them right there. He could have spoken a word to them and caused that leprosy to suddenly disappear. But He did something interesting. He said, "Go, show yourselves to the priest." Leprosy was contagious, and lepers were forbidden to be around people. They had to live in colonies, isolated from society. Jesus asked them to do something that

> *Faith says you have to believe it before you see it.*

didn't make sense, something out of the ordinary. They could have thought, *Once we're healed, once we see our skin clear up, then we'll go see the priest.* But faith says you have to believe it before you see it. You have to act like it's on the way when you don't see any sign of it.

The lepers started walking toward the priest, which could have been several miles away and taken them most of the day. I can hear people asking them, "Why are you going to the priest? You're not well. You look just the same." The first couple of hours they looked at their skin and didn't see anything different. Thoughts said, *You might as well turn around and go back home. You're just wasting your time.* But the lepers just kept on walking. There was no sign of things improving, no changes in their skin, but hour after hour they kept walking. I can imagine that at one point one of them looked at their skin and thought, *It looks like it's getting better.* Another began to move his hand and said, "My fingers are starting to function." Another exclaimed, "My skin is starting to clear up!" The Scripture says, "As they went, they were healed." If they had stayed where they were, waited for things to change, they would never have seen the miracle. The healing was in the obedience, in the going. By the time they got to the priest, they were all perfectly well.

God has put promises in your heart. He's told you that He's

restoring health to you, that you're going to lend and not borrow, that as for you and your house, you will serve the Lord. But maybe

> *You can't go by what you see or by what you don't see. Go by what God promised you.*

you're feeling like these lepers because nothing looks any different. The medical report hasn't changed, your child is still off course, and your business hasn't improved. You could get discouraged and think it's never going to happen. No, just keep walking, keep being obedient, keep praising, keep thanking. That's when the miracle is going to take place. You can't go by what you see or by what you don't see. Go by what God promised you. "Joel, I still have these symptoms." Keep on walking. "My business is still slow." Keep on walking. "People at work are still not treating me right." Keep on walking. God sees your obedience. He sees you believing when you could be discouraged. He hears you praising when you could be complaining. He sees you stretching forward when you could be shrinking back. I believe you're about to walk into your healing, walk into your freedom, walk into a great spouse, walk into abundance. As you keep walking, you're going to see God show out in your life.

It's in the Obedience

Many of the miracles Jesus performed required an act of obedience. During His first miracle, when He turned water into wine, He told the staff at the wedding to go and fill up the large stone pots with water. They had to do something that didn't make sense. They could have said, "Jesus, we need wine, not water. What good is this going to do?" The obedience is what brought the miracle. Without them filling the waterpots, there wouldn't have been any wine. Is God asking you to do something that doesn't make sense? Is He asking you to step out in faith when you don't have the experience, or to forgive that person who did you wrong, or to pray for others who need healing when you're still not feeling well? Is He asking you to bring Him five loaves and two fish when you need to feed thousands? It's not so much what you're doing; it's the obedience. When you prove to God that you're going to do the right thing even when it's hard, even when it doesn't make sense, you're going to see God do awesome things in your life.

In the Old Testament, there was a woman whose husband had died and left her in great debt. She finally ran out of funds. Now the creditors were coming to take her two sons as payment. The prophet Elisha showed up and asked her what she had in her house. She said, "I don't have anything except a small jar of olive oil." He told her to go around to her neighbors and bor-

> *Don't talk yourself out of what you know God is telling you to do.*

row as many empty containers as she could find. That didn't make sense. What good was it going to do to borrow empty containers? She could have said, "Elisha, I need full containers. I need provision. I need funds." What God asks us to do doesn't always make sense. His ways are not our ways. Many times, it's simply a test. If you obey, the miracle will follow. Don't talk yourself out of what you know God is telling you to do. Sometimes it seems ordinary. You're asking God to promote you, and He is saying, "Get to work on time and produce more than you have to." You're asking God for healing, and He is saying, "Eat healthier, exercise, and get more sleep." You're believing for your child to get back on course, and God is saying, "Help your neighbor's child. Invest in that young man." It doesn't have to make sense. That's what faith is all about.

The widow went out and borrowed all the empty containers she could. I can imagine her knocking on door after door and the neighbors thinking, *What does she need my container for? She doesn't have any food. There's no reason for it.*

> *Are you missing your miracle because you're reasoning everything out?*

But faith makes room for provision. You can't wait until it happens; you have to make room for it when you don't see any sign of it. You have to talk like it's on the way, plan like it's on the way, think like it's on the way. After working all day, she came back to her house with a couple dozen empty containers. Elisha told her to pour the little oil that she had into one of the empty containers. She could have said, "Elisha, that doesn't make sense. What good is that going to do? Why just transfer the oil from one container to the other?" But instead of talking herself out of it, she poured out that little bit of oil and kept pouring and pouring and pouring. She couldn't believe it. She filled up the first empty container, then another and another. The oil never ran out until all the containers were full. She sold the oil and not only had enough to pay the creditors, but she had plenty left over to live on. None of this would have happened if she had not been willing to do something that didn't make sense. Are you missing your miracle because you're reasoning everything out? You're looking at it all in the natural. God is supernatural. He'll ask you to do things that you may not understand.

Get Your Feet Wet

After Moses died, God raised up Joshua to lead the Israelites. The first generation of Israelites that Moses led out of slavery in Egypt never made it into the Promised Land. Because they complained and doubted, they wandered in the desert for forty years. Now the children of that generation had grown up, and Joshua was their new leader. They were headed to the Promised Land, but they had to cross the Jordan River. There were no bridges in that day. The problem was that it was the rainy season and the Jordan was in flood stage. It was over 150 feet wide, with violent currents rushing down from the melting snow on Mount Hermon. Joshua was familiar with this type of scene. When he was a young man, he was there when Moses held up his staff and the Red Sea parted. He had seen God make a way.

When the two million Israelites came to the Jordan River and saw how swollen it was and how strong the currents were, they didn't want to have anything to do with it. I can imagine Joshua did as his mentor Moses had done. He held up his rod and said, "Lord, please let these waters part." Everyone was watching with great anticipation, but nothing happened. Joshua thought, *God, this is my first test to show these people that You're really with me. Don't leave me hanging here.* God promised Joshua, "As I was with Moses, I will be with you." He didn't say, "I'm going to do for you everything I did for Moses."

> *You don't have to copy someone else and try to be what they are, try to prove your worth, try to prove that you measure up.*

God does things in different ways. You have a unique anointing. There's a distinct calling on your life. You don't have to copy someone else and try to be what they are, try to prove your worth, try to prove that you measure up. Walk in your own anointing; walk in your own calling.

The Jordan River didn't part. Joshua had to make a decision. "Are we going to turn around and go back to wandering around in the desert, or are we going to keep walking?" Joshua's attitude was: *We've come too far to stop now. God, You wouldn't have promised us this land if You weren't going to give us the victory.* Instead of turning back, Joshua put the priests out in front and told all the people, "Let's keep walking." I can hear them say, "Excuse me, Joshua, but don't you see that there's a violent raging river a few hundred feet in front of us? There's nowhere to go." Joshua acted like he didn't hear them. His instructions were, "Keep on walking." There will always be people who try to convince you to turn back. "Your dream is too big. The opposition is too strong. Nothing is working out. Just accept it." You have to do as Joshua did and have a made-up mind. "I'm going to keep walking. I'm going to become all I was created to be."

The priests got right up to the water with the ark of the covenant. It was do or die, now or never, but the waters still didn't part. They looked back at Joshua one last time, thinking, *Surely he's going to retreat now. Surely he'll come to his senses.* Joshua answered with three simple words: "Keep on walking." The Scripture says, "When the priests got in the water, when their feet got wet, suddenly the waters began to push back." All two million people went through on dry

> God is not moved by what's not moving.

ground. Miracles happen when there's obedience. God doesn't give us all the details. He doesn't show you how it's going to work out. It may not happen as you've seen happen with your family. There may not be any sign of things changing. As with Joshua, every circumstance may say, "It's not going to turn around. Go back. There's no use believing for your dreams. It's too late. You'll never get well. It would have happened by now." Don't believe those lies. Keep walking. God is not moved by what's not moving. He's not intimidated by waters that aren't parting, by how big the obstacle is, by how impossible it looks.

In fact, many times God will wait on purpose until the river is at flood stage. He'll wait until the experts say there's no way, the odds are against you, so that when He turns it around, everyone will know it was His favor, His power, and His goodness in your life. You may have situations where you don't see how it can work out in your health, your finances, or your rela-

> *Are you going to believe when you don't see any sign of things changing?*

tionships. You're tempted to quit believing. If Joshua were here today, he would tell you, "Keep walking. You're on the verge of a miracle. Those waters are about to open up." Now you may have to get your feet wet. It may not happen as it did with Moses, where the waters part first and you can see your way clearly. You know exactly how it's going to work out. Sometimes God waits to see if you're going to trust Him when the waters haven't parted. Are you going to believe when you don't see any sign of things changing? You don't feel as though you have the strength, the courage, the ability. If you just keep walking, praying, and expecting, doors are going to open that you couldn't open, healing comes that defies the odds, freedom from things that have held you back. Some Jordan Rivers are about to part. Things for which you've been standing in faith for a long time are about to come to pass. It's not going to be ordinary; it's going to be the hand of God.

When the Waters Are Not Parting

When God parted the Red Sea for Moses, the waters opened before the people went through. They could see their way clearly. It was a great miracle, but when you know where the funds are coming from, the medical report is good, or your child is excelling, that doesn't take as much faith. These people had wandered in the desert for forty years. But when God parted the Jordan River for Joshua, when the people had to get their feet wet and keep walking when it didn't look as though it was working, that group of people made it into the Promised Land. I believe it's significant. When you don't see how it can work out, but you keep walking, you keep believing, you keep being good to people, that means you're about to enter your Promised Land. God is setting you up to go where you've never been, to see favor you've never seen. Now don't complain because the water is not parting. That doesn't mean God is not going to do it. That's a sign that what He's up to is bigger than you've imagined.

You may be at the Jordan River right now. Nothing is changing. God is waiting to see if you are going to turn around and go back. "Joel, I prayed, and I believed, but my dream didn't come to pass. The people at work stopped me. I couldn't break the addiction. The waters didn't part." You're right where Joshua was. It didn't work the first time. The obstacle looks impassable. The river is swollen. The problem is bigger than it's ever been. That's a test. You have to get your feet wet. If you keep walking, you're going to see God open things up that you never dreamed would open, turn problems around you never dreamed would turn around. That Jordan River is setting you up for your Promised Land. David said, "I was young and now I'm old, yet I've never seen the righteous forsaken." He was saying in effect, "I've never seen a Jordan River that God won't part. I've never seen a sickness that He won't heal. I've never seen a dream that He won't bring to pass."

Do Not Retreat

When we were trying to acquire the Compaq Center, God gave us favor and the city council members voted for us to have the building. It had been a year-and-a-half process. Council members who were against us suddenly changed their minds and the facility was ours. As Moses did, we prayed, we believed, and God parted the Red Sea. We were grateful, and we knew it was the hand of God. But a few days after the council's approval, a company filed a lawsuit to try to keep us from moving in. They said that we violated the deed restrictions. Our attorneys told us it could be tied up in the courts for ten years. It was like we were on a roller coaster. We went from this great celebration to the reality that it might never work out. It's in times like these, when you don't see a way and the opposition is bigger and stronger, that you see what you're made of. It's easy to believe when God parts the Red Sea, but what do you do when you come to the Jordan River? You prayed, and you believed, but it didn't part. You held up your rod as your mentor did, you did what your parents did, but nothing happened. Are you going to get your feet wet? Are you going to keep walking even though thoughts tell you, *It's not going to work out. You may as well turn around. After all, God's been good to you. Be grateful for what you have?*

Don't let the enemy talk you out of your Promised Land. God has bigger things in your future. He has new mountains for you to climb. Keep walking when the waters aren't parting. Keep walking when you're not being promoted. Keep walking when your health isn't improving, when the pandemic seems like it's stopped your dreams. The reason you're facing a Jordan River at flood stage—not just a normal river, but the obstacle is bigger, more stubborn—is because your Promised Land is on the other side. You don't come to Jordan Rivers, rivers where you need to get your feet wet, if it's just another ordinary victory, something common. The Jordan means God is about to thrust you to a new level.

> *Don't let the enemy talk you out of your Promised Land.*

I woke up many times in the middle of the night when we were in that lawsuit with thoughts telling me, *You better turn around. You've told people that it's your building. You're raising funds for it. When you have to give those funds back, you're going to look like a fool. Nobody is going to listen to you.* All these voices were saying, "Retreat! The river didn't part. If God was for you, you wouldn't have this opposition. If it was going to work out, you wouldn't have this lawsuit." No, God being for you doesn't mean you won't have opposition. The enemy wouldn't be trying to stop you if you weren't a threat to him. He doesn't come against people who don't have great destinies. The reason you're facing big giants is because you're at the Jordan River. You're about to come into your Promised Land.

I didn't see how this lawsuit could ever be resolved. The other side was stubborn, but I did what I'm asking you to do: I kept on walking. When thoughts told me, *It will never work out. This company is bigger, stronger, and more influential*, I said, "Father, thank You that You're fighting our battles. Thank You that Your being for us is more than the world being against us." Our attorneys told us the other side would probably pay us a large amount of money just to go away. They

> God doesn't want you to water down your dream, to take less than what you know is in your heart.

threw out numbers with which we could practically build another facility, but we didn't want the money, we wanted the building. This building is one of the main landmarks in the city of Houston. Two million people a year came through it. It's on the main freeway and has great accessibility. We could have thought, *Let's just be safe. We may not win, so let's take the funds and go do something else.* But God doesn't want you to water down your dream, to take less than what you know is in your heart. There will always be people trying to convince you to settle. "Just accept it. You'll never get well, never break the addiction, never get out of this neighborhood." No, don't water down your dream.

You may be at the Jordan, your feet are wet, and nothing is parting. It looks like you could drown. God has not failed in the past; He's not going to start with you. Keep on walking, believing, praying, and doing the right thing. Waters are about to part, doors are about to open, and problems are about to turn around. Instead of you retreating, the opposition is going to retreat. The waters are going to push back. The sickness, the debt, the trouble is about to push back. God is going to make a way where you don't see a way.

The Miracle Is a Process

The Scripture tells us to put on the armor of God. It talks about the helmet of salvation, the breastplate of righteousness, the belt of truth, the shoes of peace, and the shield of faith. What's interesting is that there is no armor for your backside. There's nothing to cover you from the rear. That's because you

You have armor for one direction—to keep moving forward.

weren't created to retreat. You weren't created to run from opposition. You have armor for one direction—to keep moving forward. When you stand strong and fight the good fight of faith, the opposition will run from you. Psalm 114 says, "The Red Sea saw the Israelites coming and hurried out of their way." God is going to part some waters quickly. It looks as though it's going to take a long time to get well, a long time to accomplish the dream, a long time to get out of debt. No, get ready. It's going to happen sooner than you think. God is going to cause those waters, that opposition, that depression to hurry out of your way.

One day out of the blue, the other side in the lawsuit called and said they wanted to meet. We hadn't spoken to them in months, and everything was at a stalemate. They showed up, and in that one meeting

Can I tell you that we serve a big God?

they changed their mind and said we could have the building. They not only dropped the lawsuit, but they leased us nine thousand covered parking spaces. We didn't have to build our own parking structure. What happened? We came into our Promised Land. I wonder what awaits you if you just keep walking. "Well, Joel, I have some big obstacles." Can I tell you that we serve a big God? He flung stars into space, He spoke worlds into existence, and He can get you to where you're supposed to be. "The medical report says I'm not going to get well." God can do what medicine cannot do. There's not a Jordan River that He can't part. Your child may be off course, making bad choices. It looks permanent, but that is not his destiny. What God started He's going to finish.

You can stand in the gap for your children. Yes, they make their own decisions, but as parents, you have a God-given authority. When you pray, when you speak life, when you thank God that forces of darkness are broken, angels go to work. Jordan Rivers are pushed back. God hears your prayers. He sees your faithfulness. He sees you believing when you don't see things changing, thanking Him when you could be complaining. Your time is coming. Some waters are about to part. You wouldn't be reading this if God didn't have breakthroughs coming your way. Just because your feet are wet, just because you don't see anything improving, doesn't mean that it's not going to happen. God is watching you and things are going to change at the right time. The miracle is a process. It takes time, but when you come into your moment, suddenly things will turn around.

My challenge to you is that you stay in faith until you see "the suddenly." Keep on walking. The enemy always talks the loudest when you're close to the waters parting. Tune out all the negative voices and tune in to what God promised. He has spoken it, and He will bring it to pass. He wouldn't let you face a Jordan River, where your Promised Land is on the other side, if that was going to keep you from your purpose. The reason you can't see a way is because it's not going to happen naturally. God is going to do it supernaturally, things that you couldn't make happen. Don't try to figure it out. Just keep believing, keep expecting, keep doing the right thing. I believe and declare that as you keep on walking as the lepers did, you're going to see healing, favor, and promotion. Waters are about to part as they did for Joshua, new doors are about to open, and obstacles are about to come down. You're going to make it into your Promised Land.

CHAPTER FIFTEEN

Surrounded by the Most High

We all have times when we feel like we're surrounded by difficulties, surrounded by a sickness, surrounded by debt. Everywhere we turn, we're facing it. It's easy to get discouraged and think, *I'll never get out of this trouble. It has me surrounded.* That's the way a young man felt in 2 Kings 6. The king of Aram had just sent a great army with thousands of horses and chariots to surround the prophet Elisha's house. They snuck up in the middle of the night and had it totally encircled. The next morning when Elisha's assistant stepped outside and saw all the horses and chariots, he nearly passed out. He ran back in a total panic and said, "Elisha, get up! We're surrounded by the enemy. What are we going to do?" Elisha answered, "Don't be afraid. There are more for us than there are against us." I can hear the young man saying, "What do you mean? It's just you and me. I saw thousands of them." Elisha said, "Lord, open his eyes and let him see." All of a sudden, the young man looked out and saw hundreds of thousands of powerful warring angels all across the mountainside, standing with their chariots of fire. He thought he was surrounded by the enemy, but the truth is the enemy was surrounded by our God.

Like this young man, you may be surrounded by trouble, surrounded by debt, surrounded by an addiction. But what you can't see is that the Most High God is surrounding what's surrounding you. Sickness may be surrounding you, but the good news is that the sickness doesn't have the final say. Sickness is surrounded, debt is surrounded, and trouble is surrounded. Angels are working on your behalf right now. The right attitude is: *Cancer, you think you have me surrounded, but you better look again. My God has you surrounded. Debt, you think you have me surrounded. I have bad news for you. The Lord my Provider has you surrounded. Depression, you think you're going to keep me from my destiny. Trouble at work, you think you're going to stop my purpose. You may be surrounding me, and I'll give you that much. But I know a secret: The Most High God is surrounding you.* When you know God is surrounding what's surrounding you, you won't go around discouraged because of problems, worried about your finances, or upset because people are coming against you. You'll be like Elisha. You'll stay in peace, knowing the forces for you are greater than the forces against you.

> *Through your eyes of faith, you need to see every obstacle that's holding you back is surrounded by the Most High.*

Elisha prayed for the young man that God would open his eyes so he could see. There's another world that we can't see with our natural eyes. If God were to pull back the curtain as he did for this young man, and you could see into the invisible world, you would see all these forces that are for you. Powerful warring angels are at work on your behalf, standing guard, protecting you, pushing back forces of darkness. You would see God moving the wrong people out of the way, lining up things in your favor, arranging good breaks, healing, and deliverance. Don't get discouraged by what you see with your physical eyes. If you only focus on the sickness, the addiction, or the obstacle, you'll live worried and talk yourself out of your dreams. Through your eyes of faith, you need to see every obstacle that's holding you back is surrounded by the Most High.

That addiction may be strong, but it's surrounded by something stronger. God controls the universe. He flung stars into space. One angel in the Old Testament destroyed 185,000 soldiers in an army of Israel's enemies. You may have big obstacles—depression, addictions, people trying to stop you. It feels as though you're stuck. My prayer is, "God, open our eyes. Let us see that You're surrounding what's surrounding us." That child who is off track and looks as though he'll never fulfill his destiny—just imagine him surrounded by mercy, surrounded by angels, surrounded by favor. "Well, Joel, it looks to me as though he's surrounded by darkness." Yes, but if you open your eyes, you'll see that God is surrounding the darkness.

Open Your Spiritual Eyes

David said in Psalm 3, "I am not afraid of ten thousand enemies that surround me on every side." You would think that with ten thousand enemies surrounding him, David would be worried, afraid, and upset. But he went on to say, "Victory comes from you, O Lord." He was saying, "I'm surrounded by all kinds of enemies. I could be overwhelmed, but the reason I'm not falling apart is because I know

> *What you see with your physical eyes is not the only thing that's surrounding you.*

a secret: God is surrounding what's surrounding me." He had his spiritual eyes open. He didn't just see his enemies. Through his eyes of faith, he saw the Most High, fighting his battles, making his crooked places straight. As David did, you may feel surrounded by enemies, depression, sickness, and lack. Obstacles are trying to keep you from your dreams. You don't have the connections or the finances. You could easily accept it and think, *It's not meant to be.* Here's the key: What you see with your physical eyes is not the only thing that's surrounding you. If you open your eyes of faith, you'll realize that the trouble, the opposition, and the addiction are surrounded by our God. You're not just surrounded by the negative. That's one level, but God supersedes that level. You're surrounded by favor, surrounded by healing, surrounded by angels.

I saw a movie a few years ago based on a true story. An army had surrounded a city and was planning to attack it. They were very strategic to go around the whole city and make sure no one could escape. They cut off the food supply and were going to wait a few weeks until the people were starving and then go in. This army was very arrogant and cocky. Their soldiers would stand outside the city walls and shout insults and taunt the citizens, trying to get the inhabitants to engage. After about a month, they decided to attack and went rushing in full of confidence. The problem was that nobody was there. They turned around to leave and suddenly realized they were the ones who were surrounded. The people in the city had found out they were coming and had hidden and waited patiently until their moment had arrived. While the enemy army was surrounding the city, with all of their strategy and arrogance, thinking they were gaining the upper hand, the people from the city were surrounding them. When they saw they were totally surrounded, they put up the white flag, dropped their weapons, and surrendered.

When you're in a difficult time, the enemy will do a lot of talking. He'll tell you, "I have you surrounded. You're never going to get well. This sickness will be the end. You'll never break the addiction. Look how long you've had it. You'll never get out of debt. This struggle, this lack, is your destiny." Don't believe those lies. The enemy thinks he has you surrounded. What he doesn't realize is that the Most High God has him surrounded. God knows everything that's going to happen. He knows every attack, every difficulty, and every unfair situation. When you feel as though you're surrounded, you have to come back to the place of peace and say, "I know that my God is still on the throne. He's bigger than this opposition, greater than this sickness, more powerful than these enemies."

> *When you feel as though you're surrounded, you have to come back to the place of peace.*

The Fourth Man in the Fire

Remember the three Hebrew teenagers who refused to bow to King Nebuchadnezzar's golden idol in Daniel 3? Even after the king gave them one last chance to change their minds, their attitude remained: *You can't stop the plan of God for our lives. You can*

*throw us into the furnace, and the fire may surround us, but we know
our God surrounds the fire. If it's not our time to go, we're not going
to go.* They weren't upset or complaining, "God, we were doing
the right thing. Why did this happen?" They stayed in peace even
as they were cast into the fire that should have killed them imme-
diately. The amazing thing is that when the king looked into the
opening of the fiery furnace, he asked, "Didn't we throw three men
in bound? I see four men loose and one looks like the Son of God."

You may feel as though you're in the fire. Things have come
against you. You had a bad break, and you don't see how it's going
to work out. The good news is that you're not in there by yourself.
The God who controls the fire, that fourth man, He's right there with
you. That's the beauty of our God. He doesn't leave you in the tough
times. He comes into the fire with you. The king thought that throwing
them into a furnace, being surrounded

> *That's the beauty of our God. He doesn't leave you in the tough times. He comes into the fire with you.*

by fire, would surely be the end. What the king didn't realize was
that the God who created the fire, the God who controls the universe, has the final say. What's surrounding you may look powerful,
strong, and insurmountable. The good news is, our God is all-
powerful. That sickness may look like the end, but when God says
"live," you'll live. That addiction may seem permanent. Thoughts
tell you that you're never going to break it. But God is saying,
"You're not staying in that fire." That addiction is not how your
story ends. The fourth man is about to show up, and things are
about to turn in your favor. What you thought was going to stop

you is going to promote you instead. People are going to see God's blessing on your life.

When Nebuchadnezzar saw them alive in the fire, he got as close as he could and shouted, "Shadrach, Meshach, and Abednego, servants of the Most High God, come out of the fire." A few minutes earlier he was saying they had to bow down to his idol; now he was calling them servants of the Most High God. Sometimes God allows the fire just so other people will see He is God. He'll use you as an example. They may not believe before, but when they see God show out in your life, when they see you beat the cancer, when they see you break the addiction, when they see you set a new standard and go places you never dreamed, they won't be able to deny the hand of God on your life. After these teenagers came out of the fire, nobody ever looked at them the same way again. They had a new respect, a new influence, a new level. In fact, King Nebuchadnezzar said, "Praise be to the God of Shadrach, Meshach, and Abednego. There is no God like their God." Now the king was breaking his own decree and worshipping another God. He wrote a different decree that said nobody could speak a word against the God of Shadrach, Meshach, and Abednego. We may not like the fiery furnaces, but if we do as they did and keep the right attitude, we'll not only come out, but God will use that difficulty to establish us, to give us more credibility, and to take us to a new level.

They're going to see the hand of God on you.

It's interesting that the Scripture doesn't say that the teenagers could see the fourth man in the fire, the one who looked like "the Son of God." It says that Nebuchadnezzar, who had them thrown into the fire, could see Him. Don't worry about the people who try to push you down and discredit you. They're going to see the hand of God on you. Things that you may not be able to see, they're going to see. You don't have to prove to people who you are or prove to them you're right. God is your vindicator. He knows how to get their attention. He knows how to change their mind.

A Wall of Protection

"Well, Joel, if I was surrounded by the Most High, why did I have this trouble in the first place? Why didn't God keep me out of the furnace?" God never said we wouldn't have difficulties. Being a person of faith doesn't exempt us from challenges and unfair situations. They are a part of life. Psalm 34 says, "Many are the afflictions of the righteous, but the Lord will deliver us out of them all." The promise is not that you won't have difficulties; the promise is that God will bring you out—not out of some of them, not out of most of them, but out of all of them. When you're in the fire, your report should be, "I'm coming out. This sickness is temporary. This trouble is not the end. This addiction is not permanent. This slowdown in my business is just for a season." Right now, God is in the process of bringing you out. You may not be able to see it, but He's in the fire with you. Without Him, you wouldn't still be here. He's not letting those flames harm you. He's pushing back the forces of darkness. Don't complain about the fire. Give God praise in the furnace and be your best where you are. That difficulty can't keep you from your purpose. It's a test.

Remember when I wrote previously that sometimes God will

deliver us from the fire, from the difficulties, but most of the time God will make you fireproof and take you through the fire? Coming out of the furnace is a greater testimony. If God had kept the teenagers from going into the furnace, that would have been good, but coming through the fire was what gave them a new respect with the king. Their victory over the trial is what changed the way people saw them. If God kept us from every fur-

> *Coming out of the furnace is a greater testimony.*

nace, we wouldn't reach our destiny. Remember, when the teenagers were in the fire, the only thing the fire burned was the cords that bound them. Their clothes didn't burn, and their shoes didn't burn. The only thing that burned was the thing that was holding them back. When we're in the fire, God knows how to protect what we need, but burn up anything that's limiting us. You're not going to come out of the fire the same. You're going to come out stronger, free from things that were holding you back, with greater influence and greater credibility. People are going to see you in a new light. People who wouldn't give you the time of day are going to want your friendship. Those who discounted you and wouldn't consider your opinion are going to ask for your advice.

Psalm 34 says, "The angel of the Lord encamps around those who fear Him." One translation says, "God's angel sets up a circle of protection around us." That's what happened to the Hebrew teenagers. That circle of protection didn't keep them out of the fire, but it kept the fire from burning them. It was the same

> *The enemy can't break the hedge of protection that God put around you.*

thing we saw with the prophet Elisha. All those chariots of fire and warring angels had him surrounded. They formed a wall of protection. The enemy army was surrounding him in the natural, but Elisha knew that this invisible army, the angels of the Lord, were surrounding what was surrounding him. If you're not supposed to go into the fire, you're not going to go. God will keep you out. But if you do go in, it wasn't because God let you down. "I prayed, but I was thrown into the furnace. I was doing the right thing, and I came down with this illness, and my company let me go." The enemy can't break the hedge of protection that God put around you. If you go into that fire, it's because God allowed it. The good news is, the God who let you go in is the God who's going to bring you out. The enemy is not in control of your life; God is.

In the Scripture, God said to Satan, "Have you seen my servant Job? He's a man of great integrity. He honors me. There's none like him in all the land." Satan answered something interesting. He said, "Why shouldn't he honor You? You've put a hedge of protection around him." When the enemy wanted to test Job, he had to ask God for permission. Job went through those tests, those unfair situations, but he didn't get bitter. He didn't say, "Why did I get thrown into the furnace?" He said, "Though He slay me, yet will I trust Him." He was saying what the Hebrew teenagers said: "God, my life is in Your hands. I'm surrounded by difficulties, but I know You're surrounding what's surrounding me. You have the final say."

Angels Watch over You

I heard about a young lady who was walking through the parking lot to her car one night after class. It was dark and nobody was around. All of a sudden three men stepped out from where they had been hiding behind some cars. Her heart dropped, knowing they were going to harm her. She wanted to run, but she knew she didn't have a chance. She just stood there praying under her breath. These men kept coming toward her. Even though in her mind she was afraid, in her heart she felt an overwhelming peace. Something was telling her, "It's going to be okay." When those men were about fifteen feet away, they suddenly froze in their tracks. Their eyes got really big, and a look of terror came over their faces. They began to back up very slowly, very carefully. Finally, they turned around and took off running. This young lady knew that God had spared her life, but she didn't know why they turned to run.

She reported the incident to the police, and a few days later, one of the men was caught. He admitted that they were going to harm her, but he said that when they got up close, a mighty warrior appeared. I'll never forget that he used the word *warrior.* He said the angel stood over ten feet tall and that his arms and chest were rippled with muscles. The

In the unseen world right now, you have powerful warring angels surrounding you.

angel's face was radiating with so much light he could hardly look at him. He was standing over that young lady with a drawn sword in one hand and a shield in the other. He stared at those men as though he was saying, "Come on, make my day. I dare you to touch her." You're not doing life alone. In the unseen world right now, you have powerful warring angels surrounding you. You may be surrounded by trouble, but the good news is that the trouble is surrounded by the Most High. Psalm 91 says that when you honor God with your life, He will command His angels to watch over you.

Those three men thought they had that young lady surrounded. They thought it would be no problem. What was one small girl against three grown men? But what they couldn't see was the same as with Elisha. God had them surrounded. Warring angels were standing guard. Instead of going through life worried and afraid, turn it around and say, "Father, thank You that Your angels are watching over me. Thank You that I'm surrounded by protection, surrounded by favor, surrounded by goodness." When you go through life at peace, in faith, knowing that God is surrounding what's surrounding you, you're showing God that you trust Him. That's what allows Him to show Himself strong in your life.

"Joel, I have so many things coming against me. I was thrown into the fiery furnace, and I don't see how it will ever work out." That's going to keep you where you are. The right attitude is: *Yes, sickness has come against me, but I know that I'm surrounded by healing. I had a bad break, but this is not how my story ends. I'm surrounded by favor. I lost a client at work. I've had this addiction for years. My child is off course. It looks as though it's permanent, but I know a secret: I'm surrounded by increase, surrounded by freedom, surrounded by destiny.* God didn't bring you this far to leave you where you are. Those are tests.

We all get thrown into the fiery furnace. It's not to defeat you; it's to establish you. It's to let other people see that God's favor is on your life and to let you know that God is still in control. Every time God brings you through a fire, you come out with a greater trust in God, a greater confidence, a greater faith. That's getting you prepared for the next level of your destiny. With every experience, something is deposited in you that you're going to use down the road. If you didn't need the furnace, if it wasn't going to work to your advantage, God would have kept you out of it. You may not understand it, it may not seem fair, but God knows what He's doing. He's not going to let it defeat you. Thoughts will tell you, *You'll never get out. You'll never get well. It will never turn around.* Don't believe those lies. It's temporary. The furnace may be surrounding you, but God is surrounding the furnace. Right now, He's in the process of bringing you out. Things are about to change in your favor. Like those teenagers, you're not only going to come out, you're going to come out stronger and promoted to a new level.

Dare to Believe

When Elisha and his assistant were surrounded by the king of Aram's army, he prayed, "Lord, open the young man's eyes," and the young man saw the warring angels across the mountainside. But as the enemy army came closer, Elisha prayed just the opposite. He said, "Lord, make them blind," and He did. Elisha told the enemy, "You have the wrong city and are on the wrong road. Let me take you to the man you're looking for." Elisha led them to the city of Samaria, where they were surrounded by the Israelites. He then prayed, "Lord, open their eyes." They realized they were captured, and they were at Elisha's mercy. He let them go, and they stopped raiding the Israelites' territory.

God knows how to turn your situation around. As with Elisha, there are going to be enemies who are not going to bother you anymore. God is going to put an end to that sickness you've struggled with for years. The same is true for that addiction, that depression, the financial difficulty, the times when you can't seem to get ahead.

You keep doing the right thing, honoring God, being your best, and you're going to see those forces that have hindered you broken

> *There are some enemies that God is going to free you from permanently, as He did Elisha.*

once and for all. I know that we're never going to live trouble free, but there are some enemies that God is going to free you from permanently, as He did Elisha. God told the Israelites in Exodus 14, "The enemies you see today you will see no more." There are things that you're dealing with—bad habits, struggles at work, people who are against you—that are not your destiny. Dare to believe what God told the Israelites, that the depression you see today you're going to see no more, that the sickness you see today you're going to see no more, that the struggle at work, the people who are holding you back, you're going to see no more.

A salesman told me how for over twenty years he was treated unfairly at work because his boss didn't like him. He sold more than any other salesperson in the company, even though he had a smaller territory. But he was always overlooked for promotion, not given the bonuses he deserved. He kept doing the right thing. Recently, he told me, "My supervisor, the one who's been against me, was suddenly terminated." They didn't tell the staff why, saying it was private, but out of the company's sixty salespeople, he was chosen to take his supervisor's position. God is a God of justice. You keep doing the right thing, as this man did, and you'll come into that day where the enemies you see today you will see no more. They think they have you surrounded; the truth is, God has them surrounded.

My prayer is, "God, open our eyes. Let us see that there are more for us than there are against us." Sickness may have you surrounded, but keep the right perspective: God has the sickness surrounded. That trouble may be causing you to lose sleep, but come back to the place of peace. God has the trouble surrounded. You're in the palms of His hands. Sure, we all go through some fiery furnaces, but the fire is not the end. The only thing it's going to burn off is what's holding you back. All through the day remind yourself that you are surrounded by the Most High. If you do this, I believe and declare that God is going to protect you, deliver you, and promote you. Things that have held you back are being broken right now. You're going to see favor, increase, healing, restoration, and the fullness of your destiny.

ACKNOWLEDGMENTS

In this book I offer many stories shared with me by friends, members of our congregation, and people I've met around the world. I appreciate and acknowledge their contributions and support. Some of those mentioned in the book are people I have not met personally, and in a few cases, we've changed the names to protect the privacy of individuals. I give honor to all those to whom honor is due. As the son of a church leader and a pastor myself, I've listened to countless sermons and presentations, so in some cases I can't remember the exact source of a story.

I am indebted to the amazing staff of Lakewood Church, the wonderful members of Lakewood who share their stories with me, and those around the world who generously support our ministry and make it possible to bring hope to a world in need. I am grateful to all those who follow our services on television, the Internet, SiriusXM, and through the podcasts. You are all part of our Lakewood family.

I offer special thanks also to all the pastors across the country who are members of our Champions Network.

Once again, I am grateful for a wonderful team of professionals who helped me put this book together for you. Leading them is my

FaithWords/Hachette publisher, Daisy Hutton, along with team members Patsy Jones, Billy Clark, and Karin Mathis. I truly appreciate the editorial contributions of wordsmith Lance Wubbels.

I am grateful also to my literary agents Jan Miller Rich and Shannon Marven at Dupree Miller & Associates.

And last but not least, thanks to my wife, Victoria, and our children, Jonathan and Alexandra, who are my sources of daily inspiration, as well as our closest family members, who serve as day-to-day leaders of our ministry, including my mother, Dodie; my brother, Paul, and his wife, Jennifer; my sister Lisa and her husband, Kevin; and my brother-in-law Don and his wife, Jackelyn.

We Want to Hear from You!

Each week, I close our international television broadcast by giving the audience an opportunity to make Jesus the Lord of their lives. I'd like to extend that same opportunity to you. Are you at peace with God? A void exists in every person's heart that only God can fill. I'm not talking about joining a church or finding religion. I'm talking about finding life and peace and happiness. Would you pray with me today? Just say, "Lord Jesus, I repent of my sins. I ask You to come into my heart. I make You my Lord and Savior."

Friend, if you prayed that simple prayer, I believe you have been "born again." I encourage you to attend a good Bible-based church and keep God in first place in your life. For free information on how you can grow stronger in your spiritual life, please feel free to contact us.

Victoria and I love you, and we'll be praying for you. We're believing for God's best for you, that you will see your dreams come to pass. We'd love to hear from you!

To contact us, write to:

Joel and Victoria Osteen
PO Box #4271
Houston, TX 77210

Or you can reach us online at www.joelosteen.com.

Stay connected, be blessed.

Get more from Joel & Victoria Osteen

It's time to step into the life of victory and favor that God has planned for you! Featuring new messages from Joel & Victoria Osteen, their free daily devotional and inspiring articles, hope is always at your fingertips with the free Joel Osteen app and online at JoelOsteen.com.

Get the app and visit us today at JoelOsteen.com.

JOEL OSTEEN
MINISTRIES

CONNECT WITH US